First World War
and Army of Occupation
War Diary
France, Belgium and Germany

31 DIVISION
Divisional Troops
Royal Army Medical Corps
95 Field Ambulance
2 March 1916 - 31 May 1919

WO95/2354/3

The Naval & Military Press Ltd
www.nmarchive.com
Published in association with The National Archives

Published by

The Naval & Military Press Ltd

Unit 10 Ridgewood Industrial Park,

Uckfield, East Sussex,

TN22 5QE England

Tel: +44 (0) 1825 749494

www.naval-military-press.com

www.nmarchive.com

This diary has been reprinted in facsimile from the original. Any imperfections are inevitably reproduced and the quality may fall short of modern type and cartographic standards.

© Crown Copyright
Images reproduced by permission of The National Archives, London, England, 2015.

Contents

Document type	Place/Title	Date From	Date To
Heading	WO95/2354/3		
Heading	31st Division Medical 95th Field Ambulance Mar 1916-1919 May		
Heading	31st Div No. 95 F. Amb. March April 1916 Dec 18		
War Diary	Kantara	02/03/1916	02/03/1916
War Diary	Alexandria	03/03/1916	03/03/1916
War Diary	Kantara	03/03/1916	03/03/1916
War Diary	Alexandria	03/03/1916	04/03/1916
War Diary	Marseilles	06/03/1916	06/03/1916
War Diary	Alexandria	09/03/1916	09/03/1916
War Diary	Marseilles	10/03/1916	10/03/1916
War Diary	Alexandria	10/03/1916	10/03/1916
War Diary	Marseilles	09/03/1916	12/03/1916
War Diary	Liercourt	13/03/1916	14/03/1916
War Diary	Marseilles	15/03/1916	15/03/1916
War Diary	Liercourt	18/03/1916	18/03/1916
War Diary	Liercourt	16/03/1916	30/03/1916
War Diary	Bertrancourt	01/04/1916	30/04/1916
Heading	31st Div. May 1916 No. 95 F. Amb.		
War Diary	Bertrancourt	01/05/1916	12/05/1916
War Diary	Bois Du Warnimont	14/05/1916	26/05/1916
War Diary	Warnimont Wood	28/05/1916	30/05/1916
Heading	June 1916 No. 95 F.A		
War Diary	Bois Du Warnimont	01/06/1916	23/06/1916
War Diary	Bus	25/06/1916	30/06/1916
Heading	Secret.		
Operation(al) Order(s)	Operation Orders No. 1. By Lieut Colonel E.B Knox R.A.M.C.		
Heading	31st Division Vol VII War Diary Of 95th Field Amb 1st July To 31st July 1916		
War Diary	Bus-Les Artois	01/07/1916	04/07/1916
War Diary	Warnimont Wood	05/07/1916	05/07/1916
War Diary	Bernaville	06/07/1916	08/07/1916
War Diary	Robecq	09/07/1916	14/07/1916
War Diary	Vieille Chapelle	15/07/1916	31/07/1916
Heading	31st Div War Diary Of 95th FA Ambulance Aug 1916 Vol VIII		
War Diary	Vieille Chapelle	01/08/1916	29/08/1916
Heading	Cover for Documents. II. Medical Cases-Special Cases. (C) Nature of Enclosures. Glanders.		
War Diary	Vieille Chapelle	01/09/1916	30/09/1916
Heading	War Diary 95th Field Ambulance 31st Division October 1916 Volume X		
War Diary	Vieille Chapelle	01/10/1916	04/10/1916
War Diary	Zelobes	04/10/1916	05/10/1916
War Diary	Calonne	05/10/1916	08/10/1916
War Diary	Veauchelles	08/10/1916	10/10/1916
War Diary	Vauchelles	10/10/1916	17/10/1916
War Diary	Coigneux.	17/10/1916	30/10/1916

Heading	War Diary 95th Field Ambulance 31st Division November 1916. Volume. XI		
War Diary	Coigneux	01/11/1916	27/11/1916
Heading	War Diary 95th Field Ambulance 31st Division. December 1916. Volume XII		
War Diary	Coigneux.	01/12/1916	30/12/1916
Heading	War Diary 95th Field Ambulance, 31st Division January 1917 Volume XIII.		
War Diary	Coigneux	01/01/1917	10/01/1917
War Diary	Beauval	10/01/1917	31/01/1917
Heading	War Diary 95th Field Ambulance 31st Division February 1917. Volume XIV		
War Diary	Beauval	01/02/1917	20/02/1917
War Diary	Coigneux	21/02/1917	28/02/1917
Heading	War Diary 95th Field Ambulance 31st Division March 1917. Volume XV		
War Diary	Coigneux	01/03/1917	13/03/1917
War Diary	Louvencourt	18/03/1917	18/03/1917
War Diary	Sarton	19/03/1917	19/03/1917
War Diary	Fienvillers	20/03/1917	20/03/1917
War Diary	Neuvillette	21/03/1917	21/03/1917
War Diary	Pt. Houvin.	22/03/1917	22/03/1917
War Diary	Marest	24/03/1917	24/03/1917
War Diary	Fontaine-lez-Hermans.	25/03/1917	25/03/1917
War Diary	Bethune	28/03/1917	30/03/1917
Heading	War Diary 95th Field Ambulance 31st Division April 1917 Volume XVI		
War Diary	Bethune	01/04/1917	10/04/1917
War Diary	La Bourse	12/04/1917	12/04/1917
War Diary	Bajus	14/04/1917	28/04/1917
War Diary	Ecoivres	29/04/1917	29/04/1917
War Diary	St. Catherine	30/04/1917	30/04/1917
Heading	###		
Miscellaneous	95th F.A. 31st Divn. 13th Corps. O.C. Lt. Col. C.B. Knox. 1st Army. 3rd Army From 11/4/17	11/04/1917	11/04/1917
Heading	War Diary 95th Field Ambulance 31st Division May 1917. Volume XVII		
War Diary	St. Catherine	01/05/1917	21/05/1917
War Diary	Cambligneul.	24/05/1917	29/05/1917
Heading	###		
Miscellaneous	95th F.A. 31st Divn. 13th Corps. O.C. Lt. Col. C.B. Knox. 3rd Army.		
Heading	War Diary 95th Field Ambulance 31st Division June 1917 Volume XVIII		
War Diary	Cambligneul	01/06/1917	10/06/1917
War Diary	Anzin	11/06/1917	30/06/1917
Heading	War Diary 95th Field Ambulance 31st Division July 1917 Volume XIX		
War Diary	Anzin	01/07/1917	02/07/1917
War Diary	Maroeuil	04/07/1917	31/07/1917
Heading	War Diary 95th Field Ambulance 31st Division August 1917 Volume XX		
War Diary	Maroeuil	01/08/1917	31/08/1917
Heading	War Diary 95th Field Ambulance 31st Division September 1917. Volume XXI		
War Diary	Maroeuil	01/09/1917	13/09/1917

War Diary	Anzin	13/09/1917	29/09/1917
Heading	Volume XII War Diary 95th Field Ambulance 31st Division October 1917		
War Diary	Anzin	01/10/1917	26/10/1917
Heading	Volume XXIII War Diary 95th Field Ambulance 31st Division November 1917		
War Diary	Anzin	01/11/1917	30/11/1917
War Diary	Volume XXII War Diary. 95th Field Ambulance 31st Division December 1917		
War Diary	Anzin	01/12/1917	28/12/1917
Heading	Jan 1918 No 95. F.A.		
War Diary	Anzin	01/01/1918	30/01/1918
Heading	Feb 1918 No 95. F.A.		
War Diary	Anzin	01/02/1918	28/02/1918
Heading	Mar. 1918. 95th Field Amb.		
War Diary	Anzin	01/03/1918	01/03/1918
War Diary	Houvelin	02/03/1918	22/03/1918
War Diary	Blaireville	23/03/1918	25/03/1918
War Diary	Bailleulmont	25/03/1918	25/03/1918
War Diary	La Cauchie	26/03/1918	31/03/1918
Heading	Apr 1918. 160/2902 1st Field Amb		
War Diary	Lacauchie	01/04/1918	01/04/1918
War Diary	Warluzel	02/04/1918	02/04/1918
War Diary	Tincques	04/04/1918	07/04/1918
War Diary	Aubigny	07/04/1918	10/04/1918
War Diary	Strazeele	11/04/1918	12/04/1918
War Diary	Hondeghem	13/04/1918	19/04/1918
War Diary	Wallon Cappel	20/04/1918	27/04/1918
War Diary	Hondeghem (Sheet 27 V.4.c.2.6)	28/04/1918	30/04/1918
Heading	Volume XXIX War Diary 95th Field Ambulance May, 1918		
War Diary	Hondeghem	01/05/1918	24/05/1918
War Diary	Beaumont	24/05/1918	30/05/1918
Heading	June 1918 95th F.A.		
War Diary	Beaumont	01/06/1918	07/06/1918
War Diary	Lannoy Chateau, Nr. Lumbres.	08/06/1918	21/06/1918
War Diary	Wallon Cappel.	22/06/1918	24/06/1918
War Diary	Ebblinghem	25/06/1918	30/06/1918
Heading	July 1918. 95th. F.A.		
War Diary	Ebblinghem	01/07/1918	31/07/1918
Heading	Aug. 1918. 95th F. Amb		
War Diary	Ebblinghem	01/08/1918	23/08/1918
War Diary	Caestre	24/08/1918	31/08/1918
Heading	Sept 1918 95th Fd. Amb.		
War Diary	Fletre	01/09/1918	04/09/1918
War Diary	Bailluel	05/09/1918	10/09/1918
War Diary	Fletre	12/09/1918	30/09/1918
Heading	Oct 1918 No 95 F.A.		
War Diary	Fletre	01/10/1918	16/10/1918
War Diary	Carlisle Lines.	17/10/1918	17/10/1918
War Diary	Quesnoy	18/10/1918	18/10/1918
War Diary	Lannoy	19/10/1918	26/10/1918
War Diary	Staceghem	27/10/1918	31/10/1918
Heading	Nov 1918 No 95 F.A.		
War Diary	Staceghem	01/11/1918	02/11/1918
War Diary	Reckem.	03/11/1918	09/11/1918

War Diary	Avelghem.	10/11/1918	13/11/1918
War Diary	Reckem	14/11/1918	24/11/1918
War Diary	Vlamertinghe	25/11/1918	25/11/1918
War Diary	Steenvoorde	26/11/1918	26/11/1918
War Diary	Le Nieppe	27/11/1918	27/11/1918
War Diary	St. Martin Au Laert	28/11/1918	30/11/1918
Heading	Dec. 1918 No 95 F.A.		
War Diary	St Martin Au Laert	01/12/1918	14/12/1918
War Diary	Leulinghem	17/12/1918	30/12/1918
War Diary	Wisques	31/12/1918	31/12/1918
Heading	Jan 1919 31 Div Box 2131 No 95 Field Ambulance		
War Diary	Wisques	01/01/1919	31/01/1919
Heading	Jan 1919 95 7.a. 160/3551		
War Diary	Wisques	01/01/1919	31/01/1919
Heading	Feb 1919 No. 95 Field Ambulance		
War Diary	Wisques	01/02/1919	28/02/1919
Heading	Apr 1919 95th F.a. 140/3550		
War Diary	Malasise	01/04/1919	30/04/1919
Heading	May 1919 No 95 Field Ambulance		
War Diary	Malasise	01/05/1919	31/05/1919

W095/23543

31ST DIVISION
MEDICAL

95TH FIELD AMBULANCE
MAR 1916 - DEC 1918
1919 MAY

Left Kantara
3.3.16

3 Poko Bu

March } 1916
April }

JB. 95 F. Ount

COMMITTEE FOR THE
MEDICAL HISTORY OF THE WAR
Date 9 JUN 1916

No. 1 March 1916

Army Form C. 2118.

WAR DIARY
or
INTELLIGENCE SUMMARY

(Erase heading not required.)

Instructions regarding War Diaries and Intelligence Summaries are contained in F. S. Regs., Part II. and the Staff Manual respectively. Title pages will be prepared in manuscript.

Place	Date	Hour	Summary of Events and Information	Remarks and references to Appendices
KANTARA	2.3.16		LIEUT. L.M. INGLE, LIEUT. A.R. ELLIOTT, LIEUT. H.H. MATHIAS and LIEUT. E.C. CUNNINGTON, together with 5 Batmen left KANTARA for ALEXANDRIA from Kantara for B.E.F. FRANCE.	
ALEXANDRIA	3.3.16		Re above officers and Men embarked on H.T. "CESTRIAN" for B.E.F. FRANCE.	
KANTARA	3.3.16		"A" and "B" Sections (3 officers and 136 N.C.Os and Men R.A.M.C and A.S.C.) left KANTARA for ALEXANDRIA to embark for B.E.F. FRANCE.	
ALEXANDRIA	3.3.16		"A" Section (LIEUT-COLONEL E.B. KNOX, LIEUT W. HUNT and 71 N.C.Os and Men R.A.M.C and A.S.C. embarked on H.M.Y.S. "NESSIAN" for B.E.F. FRANCE.	
			"B" Section (LIEUT. C.W. WEST and 59 N.C.Os and Men R.A.M.C.) arrived at GABBARI REST CAMP ALEXANDRIA to await embarkation for B.E.F. FRANCE.	
	4.3.16		5 Officers 15 Batmen, also "A" Section moved off from Quay on H.T. "NESSIAN" but returned & disembarked, stayed night (A.S.L.) moved off	
	6.3.16		"C" Section (LIEUT. A. & WINTER, LIEUT. H. YOUNG and 46 N.C.Os and men R.A.M.C.) left "KARGA" for B.E.F. FRANCE from PORT SAID and disembarked for B.E.F.	
MARSEILLES	6.3.16		"B" Section to GABBARI REST CAMP and entrained at ___ for B.E.F.	
ALEXANDRIA	9.3.16		5 Officers and 5 Men disembarked for B.E.F.	
MARSEILLES	10.3.16		"B" Section moved off from Quay and rail as above named	
ALEXANDRIA			"B" Section entrained by train for about 2 days, and arrived at	
MARSEILLES	9/10.3.16		from MARSEILLES "C" Section billeted for the night, and marched next day ABBEVILLE on 9.3.1916. No "A" Section stayed for LIERCOURT to LIERCOURT, arriving same day.	
MARSEILLES	12.3.16		"A" Section disembarked and entrained for LIERCOURT	
LIERCOURT	13.3.16		5 officers min (above mentioned) arrived, and joined up with "C" Section.	
	14.3.16		"A" Section arrived from MARSEILLES.	
MARSEILLES	15.3.16		"B" Section disembarked for B.E.F. and billeted overnight in the Railway shed	
LIERCOURT	16.3.16		"B" Section arrived from MARSEILLES after entraining on 16.3.16	

No. 2. March 1916

Army Form C. 2118.

WAR DIARY
or
INTELLIGENCE SUMMARY.
(Erase heading not required.)

Instructions regarding War Diaries and Intelligence Summaries are contained in F. S. Regs., Part II. and the Staff Manual respectively. Title pages will be prepared in manuscript.

Place	Date	Hour	Summary of Events and Information	Remarks and references to Appendices
LIERCOURT	18.3.16		M. DEMASURE (French Interpreter) reported for duty and was added to the strength	
"	16.3.16		68094 Pte Brown W. transferred from No.2 Stationary Hospital and was added to the strength.	
			68506 Sgt Porter W.C. admitted to Hospital at Marseilles (14.3.16) and reported sick on arrival of "B" Section at LIERCOURT	
			68594 Pte G.W. Killingbeck was discharged from Hospital 6.3.16. He embarked at PORT SAID and disembarked MARSEILLES with of a Battalion of 4 officers and reported to this Unit 18.3.16 and was added to the strength of the Unit	
"	19.3.16		1 Sergeant and 1 Private proceeded for 8 days furlough	
			68894 Lce/Cpl Spencer E.J transferred to No.2 Stationary Hospital	
"	20.3.16		LIEUT E.C CUNNINGTON proceeded to duty with 13th Batt East Yorks	
"	21.3.16		5 Privates reported themselves arrived from 12th (S) Bn John Thanes, and were added to the strength.	
			2 Officers & 38 Other ranks proceeded on 8 days furlough	
"	22.3.16		2 Officers & 3 O/Rs proceeded for duty to 108th Field Ambulance for NEEVILLE for instructions	
			3 M.C.Cs and 13 Men, 4 Motor Ambulances, and 3 Motor Bicycles arrived from 31st Field Ambulance Workshop Unit	
"	23.3.16		68543 Pte Riffle transferred to No.2 Casualty Clearing Station	
"	24.3.16		Instructions to Unit to move to New area 27/25 inst. were given	
"	25.3.16		The whole Ambulance left LIERCOURT (by road) and arrived FLESSELLES same day	
	26.3.16		FLESSELLES	
	27.3.16		BEAUVAL	
			VAUCHELLES	

No 3 March 1916.

Army Form C. 2118.

WAR DIARY
or
INTELLIGENCE SUMMARY.

(Erase heading not required.)

Instructions regarding War Diaries and Intelligence Summaries are contained in F. S. Regs., Part II. and the Staff Manual respectively. Title pages will be prepared in manuscript.

Place	Date	Hour	Summary of Events and Information	Remarks and references to Appendices
	28.3.16		Advance Party left VAUCHELLES.	
	30.3.16		28.3.1916 for duty at Brewery Stations at MAILLY. The remainder of Ambulance left VAUCHELLES and arrived BERTRANCOURT same day	

C B Kent
Lieut-Colonel, R.A.M.C.
Commanding,
95th Field Ambulance,
31st Division.

WAR DIARY or INTELLIGENCE SUMMARY

Army Form C. 2118.

Place	Date	Hour	Summary of Events and Information	Remarks and references to Appendices
BERTRANCOURT	1.4.16		1 French Interpreter and 5 Men (comprising a French Guard Section) were added to the strength for rations, etc. Also 3 men of R.E. Pigeon Section.	
	2.4.16		M2. 152406 Cpl Bacon J.W. (Motor Transport) transferred to Mob. Barracks Beavery Division. M2. 133007 Pte Ballard W.H.C., M2. 048069 Pte Bleaden R.B. (Motor transport) transferred from the 31st Field Ambulance Workshop Unit. M.2.153100 Cpl Rear O.D. and H.6.0.s and men proceeded for 8 days furlough.	
	3.4.16		2 N.C.Os. proceeded for 8 days furlough.	
	6.4.16		5 Riding Horses were transferred from 93rd Field Ambulance.	
	7.4.16		1012 Pte Taylor H.Y. 821, Pte Taylor A.H.Y. 835, Pte Hayden A.B.J., 826 Pte Eyres W. transferred from 4/1st Monmouthy Section.	
			Advanced Dressing Station at MAILLY-MAILLET and AUCHONVILLIERS were handed over to Field Ambulance of 29th Division and detachment regained regimental unit at BERTRANCOURT.	
	8.4.16		3 Officers, 11 other Ranks and 5 Horses of G.O. R.G.A. were attached for rations. HH3 Cpl Remington 3396 Cpl Muston, 7408 Bee Carter, 8131 Cpl Parker 5489 Pte Winters M.M. Police transferred from A.P.M. 31st Division.	
	11.4.16		LIEUT. E.C. CUNNINGTON returned from duty with 13 BATT. EAST YORKS REGT LIEUT L.M. INGE proceeded to COURCELLES to act as Town Commandant LIEUT. E.C. CUNNINGTON proceeded to duty as Medical Officer i/c 10TH EAST YORKS REGT.	
	14.4.16		The under mentioned N.C.O. & men were transferred to Mot Batteries (Ambulance Convoys) (9th Division). 68540 Pte Q.M.S. Little G. transferred to Mot. Batteries Clearing Station.	
	18.4.16		54997 Pte Louston N, 6039 Pte Ray Haywards W transferred from 25TH FIELD AMBULANCE 15 men were engaged in the atterification of water by means of Chloride of Lime.	
	20.4.16		68523 Pte Coal H.H. transferred to No 30 Casualty Clearing Station	
	21.4.16		LIEUT. E.C. CUNNINGTON returned from duty with 6.10/EAST YORKS REGT.	

Sheet No 2 April 1916.

WAR DIARY
or
INTELLIGENCE SUMMARY.
(Erase heading not required.)

Army Form C. 2118.

Place	Date	Hour	Summary of Events and Information	Remarks and references to Appendices
BEAURAINCOURT	21.4.16		3296 Pte Bolton M.M.P. transferred to A.P.M. 31st Division. 1568 Bpl Lowden M.M.P. transferred from A.P.M. 31st Division	
	22.4.16		Lieut W. Hunt took over Medical charge of 12th Batt. York & Lancs. Regt (Matn) 49309 Pte Mann & 49099 Pte Be S Lowsley, 80516 Pte Miller & 49331 Pte Noyes transferred from No 5 General Base Depot.	
	23.4.16		1938 Driver Scott J.B. transferred to No 29 Casualty Clearing Station	
	24.4.16		Lieut W. Hunt and Lieut C.M. West were transferred to the rank of Captain.	
	26.4.16		Inflew and 2 Men proceeded to 1st Stage furlough	
	27.4.16		Capt W. Hunt handed over medical charge of 12th Batt York & Lancs Regt to Lieut G.O. Summerton. Lieut H Young transferred to 2nd in Brigade becoming R.O. 10th 3 Men of 7cc R&A attached to rotation 26 M 16, 0.16 to 10 men Bn 24.4.16 4413 L/Cpl Hemingway M.M.P. transferred to A.P.M. 31st Division 10411 Sac W/J Bunger M.M.P. transferred from A.P.M. 31st Division.	
	28.4.16		3 Men of 10 R.G.A. attached temporarily. M. DEMASURE (French Interpreter) transferred to 15th Army Corps.	
	29.4.16			
	30.4.16		M. DURALLET (French Interpreter) transferred from 93rd Field Ambulance for duty	

E B Knox
Lieut-Colonel, R.A.M.C.
Commanding,
95th Field Ambulance,
31st Division.

31st Dev.

May 1915

No. 95 7. Aust.

COMMITTEE FOR THE
MEDICAL HISTORY OF THE WAR
Date 26 JUN 1915

WAR DIARY or INTELLIGENCE SUMMARY

Army Form C. 2118.

No. 1. May 1916

Place	Date	Hour	Summary of Events and Information	Remarks and references to Appendices
BERTRANCOURT	1.5.16		G.O.C. R.G.A. + 2 other ranks attached for rations.	
			66001 Pte Durbrow C.H. transferred to No.13 General Hospital for dental treatment.	
			108685 Pte Kelly G. & former biologist, with boy at 9, for her client.	
			6146 Pte Brighton E. & 9776 Pte Lucas G. 54966 Pte Smith W.R., 16215 Pte Hawkes R.S.	
	2.5.16		5914 Pte Burbury B. transferred to COUIN. (French Leave Section).	
			G.O.C. R.G.A. & other ranks struck off strength for rations.	
			Cpl Rafferty, Pte Bell, Pte Finger (R.E. Pigeon Section) transferred to LAVIEVILLE,	
			SENLIS and CORBIE respectively.	
			CAPT. C.M. WEST proceeded to CORBELLES to assume medical charge of 1/6 th WEST YORKS REGT.	
	3.5.16		G.O.C. R.G.A. 30 other ranks attached for rations	
			1568 CPL LOWDEN, 3296 CPL BURTON, 4108 CPL CARTER, 8134 CPL BARKER, MM POLICE Staff Sergeant	
			to Headquarters at B.U.S.	
			5943 SGT FEEK A, 5553 CPL YATES G, 7965 CPL WEBSTER T, 8045 CPL HARPER M.M POLICE	
			transferred from Headquarters at BUS for duty.	
			G.O.C. R.G.A. 2 other ranks attached for rations.	
	4.5.16		66890 Pte BALL W.T. allowed working pay at the rate of 1/- per diem as Laundryman.	
			71145 CPL CALLOW F.A. 68545 Pte STALEY B, 68514 Pte MILLS W.A transferred to H.Q. N21.	
	6.5.16		M DURALLET (French Interpreter) transferred to AMIENS	
			HEAVY ARTILLERY GROUP BEAUSSART for duty.	
			M DURALLET (French Interpreter) transferred from South Midland C.C.S.	
	7.5.16		LIEUT H. YOUNG discharged from hospital returned with pay.	
	8.5.16		PTE. TAYLOR F. promoted to acting unpaid Lance Corporal. Diarea N.Y.D.	
	9.5.16		LIEUT H. MATHIAS admitted Hopt. Blanely & Leering Evacuation Diarea N.Y.D.	
	10.5.16		2 Subs and 20 other ranks moved to the B.U.S. do WARNIMONT on the BUS-AUTHIE road as	
	(12.5.16)		advance party to make new camp ground	

Sheet No. 2. May 1916

Army Form C. 2118.
1 JUN 1916

Instructions regarding War Diaries and Intelligence Summaries are contained in F.S. Regs., Part II. and the Staff Manual respectively. Title pages will be prepared in manuscript.

WAR DIARY
of
INTELLIGENCE SUMMARY.
(Erase heading not required.)

Place	Date	Hour	Summary of Events and Information	Remarks and references to Appendices
GERTRANCOURT	12.5.16		Remainder of Ambulance left for new camp in BOIS DU WARNIMONT.	
BOIS DU WARNIMONT	14.5.16		1 Heavy Draught Riding Horse died.	
	15.5.16		G.O.C. R.G.A allowed 4 pouch oft. through 1st through for 8 days furlough.	
			1 N.C.O. proceeded for 8 days furlough.	
			CAPT. C.M. WEST carried on duty with 16th WEST YORKS REGT. as MEDICAL OFFICER	
			LIEUT-COL. E.B. KNOX proceeded on Annual Leave and at 30.5.1916	
			83951 SPR. T. BROWN 211th Coy R.E. attached for duty.	
			10 Men from 12th YORKS and LANCS (isolation co.co) attached for rations only	
			1 A.S.C. Farrier proceeded for 8 days furlough.	
			TH/160123 Dr BREWEN E. and TH/160419 Dr JOHNSON W.M. transferred from 31st Divisional	
	16.5.16		Train A.B. and are ordered to Hesdingneul.	
			1 Light Draught Horse returned by No.2 SIEGE CO. R.E.	
	17.5.16		1 Riding Horse transferred to 4th MOBILE VETERINARY HOSPITAL	
			1 N.C.O. and 1 Private proceeded for 8 days furlough.	
			LIEUT H YOUNG proceeded to BUS to take charge of Divisional Baths.	
*	18.5.16		LIEUT A G WINTER proceeded to take over Medical charge of 18TH DURHAM LIGHT INFANTRY	
	19.5.16		1 A.S.C. Driver + 1 R.A.M.C. Private proceeded for 8 days furlough.	
			3 N.C.O.S and 6 men proceeded to BUS for duty with supplies in charge Baths	
	20.5.16		1 Riding Horse transferred from 31st DIVISION D.A.C.	
	21.5.16		2 Men proceeded on 8 days furlough.	
			LIEUT L.N. INGLE returned from duty as Army Commandant COURCELLES	
	23.5.16		83951 SPR. T BROWN 211TH CO. R.E. returned to his unit	
*	16.5.16		MAJOR-GENERAL R WANLESS-O'GOWAN and staff inspected the camp.	
			D.D.M.S and A.D.M.S 31st Division inspected the camp.	
	19.5.16		6854H PTE. SMULLEN P. transferred to Mob. Casualty Clearing Station	
	26.5.16		6939H PTE CAMPBELL A. transferred from No.5. General Base Depot and was ordered to Hesdingneul.	

Unit No. 3   May 1916.

Army Form C. 2118.

WAR DIARY
or
INTELLIGENCE SUMMARY.
(Erase heading not required.)

Place	Date	Hour	Summary of Events and Information	Remarks and references to Appendices
WARNIMONT WOOD	28.5.16		LIEUT. L.M. INGUS proceeded to PONT NOYELLES for duty course at Fourth Army Anti-Gas School.	
			65619 L/C F.W. McLEOD and 68119 L/C TERRY A.L. were found to 93rd Field Ambulance for eye treatment.	
			The following were transferred to 9?th. Brigade Machine Gun Co. and to a much attle strength T/5R/3604 Pte Watts H T/M1039404 Pte Boynes J were posted to 31st Divisional Train and one Driver J Pike brought	
	30.5.16		One Boy was admitted to H.B. Hubele recovery the pink A Melbourne V.R15 LIEUT-COL E.B. KNOX returned from divisional Zgave.	

E V Knox
Lieut.-Colonel, R.A.M.C.
Commanding,
95th Field Ambulance,
31st Division.

1 JUN 1916
95TH FIELD AMB.
A.M.C.

June 1916
S.

cRo. 95 J.Q.

COMMITTEE FOR THE
MEDICAL HISTORY OF THE WAR
Date 5 AUG. 1915

Sheet 1. June 1916.

Army Form C. 2118.

WAR DIARY
INTELLIGENCE SUMMARY.

(Erase heading not required.)

Instructions regarding War Diaries and Intelligence Summaries are contained in F.S. Regs., Part II. and the Staff Manual respectively. Title pages will be prepared in manuscript.

1 JUL 1916 R.A.M.C.

Place	Date	Hour	Summary of Events and Information	Remarks and references to Appendices
BOIS DU WARNIMONT	1.6.16		S. GENERAL. A.T. SLOGGETT visited and inspected the Camp.	
	3.6.16		LIEUT L.M INGLE returned from course at Anti-Gas-School PONT NOYELLES	
			PTE LEAR H discharged from NO 2 STATIONARY HOSPITAL.	
	5.6.16		The D.D.M.S and MAJOR BOYLAN SMITH visited and inspected the Camp	
			1 section comprising 2 officers 60 H.O's and W.R.A.M.L 10 H.B.O's and M.U.O A.S.C, 2 Army M.T. A.S.C and transport proceeded to GEZAINCOURT for duty.	
			153100 £60 A O REENE. M.T.A.S.C. transferred to 31st Divisional Train by way column.	
			M2/035230 Sgt T. McQUONE. M.T.A.S.C. transferred from 3rd Divisional Supply Column	
			69059 PTE A M MORRIS transferred to No 10 H. CASUALTY CLEARING STATION	
			LIEUT. J.W. MACFARLANE transferred from No 4 GENERAL HOSPITAL and LIEUT A. MAC CAWLEY	
			transferred from NO 10 STATIONARY HOSPITAL.	
	6.6.16		LIEUT. A McCAWLEY proceeded to ORVILLE to take over Medical Charge and sanitation of Town.	
	7.6.16		M2/153209 L/Cpl. H. MATTHEWS transferred to 31st Divisional Column by return, a Lieu / Motor Cycle.	
			LIEUT. A.G. WINTER handed over Medical & Charge of 18 DURHAM LIGHT INFANTRY to LIEUT T.W. MACFARLANE	
	11.6.16		SGT. F.W LOCKLEY proceeded to attend a course of instructions in Anti-Gas Measures at BUS.	
	13.6.16.		Section returned from duty at GEZAINCOURT.	
	15.6.16		12304 PTE. C.W ORAN transferred from 13th Field Ambulance +62551 Rr W. MORRIS transferred from 93rd Field Ambulance.	
	14.6.16		MAJOR BOYLAN SMITH visited and inspected the Camp.	
	20.6.16		2 officers and 30 other ranks with Horses sent proceeded for duty at GEZAINCOURT.	
	22.6.16		1966 PTE. C.F WOOD transferred from 31st Field Ambulance.	
	23.6.16		CAPT G. MITCHELL transferred from VIII CORPS TROOPS and is ordered to take charge	
			"A" section consisting of 6 officers + 58 other ranks R.A.M.L, 30 Keep with M.T A.S.C proceeded to BUS.	

2353 Wt. W2544/1454 700,000 5/15 D.D.&L. A.D.S.S./Forms/C. 2118.

WAR DIARY
INTELLIGENCE SUMMARY
(Erase heading not required.)

Army Form C. 2118.

95. F amb
Vol 4
June

Stamp: 95 FIELD AMBULANCE, 1 JUL 1916, R.A.M.O.

Month & Year: June 1916.

Instructions regarding War Diaries and Intelligence Summaries are contained in F. S. Regs., Part II and the Staff Manual respectively. Title pages will be prepared in manuscript.

Place	Date	Hour	Summary of Events and Information	Remarks and references to Appendices
BUS.	25.6.16		Detachment on duty at GEZAINCOURT returned to BUS, and their places filled to WARNIMONT WOOD. "C" Section moved from WARNIMONT WOOD to BUS.	
	26.6.16		G.8 & 23 PTE A. HILL transported to give Field Ambulance and is struck off the strength. The D.D.M.S and A.D.M.S visited and inspected the camp.	
	28.6.16		LIEUT A. MAR CAWLEY proceeds to duty as M.O. with 15th West Yorks Regt. LIEUT A.R. ELLIOTT seconded to 93rd Field Ambulance supplying some officers. 39 M.C. O.R's orderlies transferred from 93rd Field Ambulance to us. PTE T.M. HIGKINBOTHAM transferred from "C" Coy SOUTHCAMP RUBN for duty as Reinforcement.	
	29.6.16		"B" "C" Sections returned to WARNIMONT WOOD.	
	30.6.16		"A" "B" & "C" Stretcher Bearer Sections proceeded to COLINCAMPS for duty.	

E.R. Kume
Lieut-Colonel, R.A.M.O.
Commanding,
95th Field Ambulance,
31st Division.

SECRET.

OPERATION ORDERS No. 1. 95th Field Ambulance. R.A.M.C.

By Lieut Colonel E. B. Knox R.A.M.C.

Reference MAP FRANCE 57D. N.E. 1.20000.

(1). <u>Personnel</u> will be distributed as follows:—

   <u>TENT SUB DIVISION.</u>

     A. under Captain MITCHELL at BUS.

     C. under Lieut. WINTER at BUS.
     as Main Dressing Station.

     B. under Captain HUNT at WARNIMONT WOOD, which will act as a Reserve Main Dressing Station.

   <u>BEARER SUB DIVISIONS.</u>

These will be under the command of Captain WEST and he will be assisted by Lieut INGLE. They will remove wounded from the 93rd. Brigade on the right sector of the attack — The O.C. Bearer Sub Divisions will arrange early with the Town Major COLINCAMPS for the accommodation of the bearers assigned to that Station. Billet No. 50 (next to the Advanced Dressing Station) has been set aside for this purpose — The QUARTERMASTER, 95th Field Ambulance will arrange for water and rations to be sent to these Bearers each night. Stretcher Squads will consist of three men with one Surgical Haversack, one Haversack of Shell dressings, and one Water bottle. Reserve stretchers, 20 will be kept at EUSTON and 10 at COLINCAMPS. All French stretchers will be brought forward to EUSTON and employed in carrying wounded from the front line.

No. 2.

<u>O.C. BEARER SUB-DIVISIONS</u> will arrange for his Bearers to be in positions already assigned to them by 1-30 a.m. on Z day.

Strict orders will be issued that:—

    (a) Perfect silence must be maintained on the road in the trenches.

    (b) No smoking or lights will be permitted after leaving billets.

    (c) Ranks must be well closed up on the march.

    (d) The R.A.M.C. Stretcher squads are not to go into the trenches in front of the Regimental Aid Posts, unless under orders of O.C. Bearer Sub Divisions.

Each bearer will carry his Ground sheet, Waterbottle, Haversack, and wear his steel helmet.—

One days ration and Iron ration to be carried.—

Greatcoats, blankets and packs will be handed over to the QUARTER MASTER'S Store.

C.C. TENT SUB-DIVISIONS.

The Officer in charge Main Dressing Station will take steps only to receive and treat Wounded, and no other cases will be entered in the Admission and Discharge Book. All sick to be sent to 93rd. Field Ambulance for direct admission. All wounded on arrival will be classified by the MEDICAL OFFICER who takes them over as lying down or sitting cases and grouped in huts accordingly for evacuation. Serious cases and cases not to be moved will be kept in one hut. Wounded cases who have received Antitetanic injections at the Advanced Dressing Stations will have a X marked on the back of their left or right wrist, Wounded not so marked will be given an injection at the Tent Section here, and the back of the left wrist so marked with an indelible pencil, and also an entry T (with number of Units given 500 as a rule) on the back of their tally. All cases dressed and attended to at the Advanced Dressing Stations will have D marked in the corner of the tally, and these cases will probably require not immediate further dressing. Cases marked DX. are those which will probably require further dressing. Cases marked "Tourniquet" will mean that a tourniquet is in position.

No. 14.

REPORTS AND RETURNS.

The present routine messages and reports will continue to be sent as hitherto fore —. In addition the following messages are required to be sent to the A.D.M.S. so as to reach his office without fail at the hours stated:—

(1). Number of Wounded only.

    A. admitted to each Field Ambulance between.

        6 a.m. and Noon, reach A.D.M.S. 11.45 a.m.
        Noon and 9 P.M.   " A.D.M.S. 8.45 P.M.
        9 P.M. and 6 A.M.   " A.D.M.S. 5.45 A.M.

Officers, French troops and prisoners of war to be distinguished.

    B. Remaining in each Field Ambulance distinguishing "Lying down" and "Sitting" cases thus:—

"A.D.M.S. 31st Division. No... 26th. June A.A.A. admitted since 6 a.m. 95th. Field Ambulance, Officers 10, Other Ranks 120, French 2, Germans 3, A.A.A. Remaining lying 40, Sitting 95. A.A.A. Officers names not required. Numbers for Divisional Collecting Stations will be included in the report from the Field Ambulance to which they belong.— When these cases are being sent to the Corps Collecting Station at ACHEUX, a note will be made on the tally of each case to the effect that they are transferred.

No. 5.

RETURNS.

The following return based on this classification (see orders, No.4) will be rendered to ORDERLY ROOM three times daily, at 5 a.m., 11 a.m. and 8 P.M. without fail:—

"To O.C. 95th. Field Ambulance"
No.... dated.... A.A.A. Admitted since 8 P.M. Officers, Other ranks, French, Germans. A.A.A. Remaining lying, sitting.
(Officers names Regiments etc should be given).

USE of ARMY FORM W3210.

As each case is received in the Reception Room or Ward his particulars are entered on Army Form W3210, a serial number being stamped on both portions of the Army Form. The smaller portion is then detached and pinned to the patients coat or shirt which denotes that his particulars have been taken.

The book of Army Forms W3210 after all the patients particulars have been taken is then returned to the Office and the necessary entries are made in the Admission and Discharge book from the particulars which have been obtained on the Army Form.

When the patient is evacuated the number portion of the Army Form which was pinned to his coat or shirt on admission is taken from him as he leaves the ward or building, and placed in a bag or some receptacle for the purpose which is eventually taken to the Office when the necessary entry is made in the A and D book against the serial number quoted on the ticket.

No. 5. Continued.

EVACUATIONS.

Lying down cases to No.11 and No.29. Casualty Clearing Stations by No. 20 Motor Ambulance Convoy.

Sitting cases sitting and lying by Corps Collecting Station ACHEUX, thence by Light Railway to Casualty Clearing Station. Cases for Divisional Collecting Station will be sent under Divisional arrangements to Corps Collecting Station.

OFFICERS.

As far as possible Wounded Officers will be sent to GEZAINCOURT, but all Casualty Clearing Stations can receive them.

SPECIAL CASES.

Abdominal and other injuries requiring immediate operation will be sent to 1/2 South Midland Field Ambulance. AUTHIE.

No. 6.

TRANSPORT.

The Motor Transport from the Advanced Dressing Stations will be under the O.C. 94th. Field Ambulance, who will be responsible for its distribution. Four Siddeley-Deasy cars and one Ford will be supplied by the 95th. Field Ambulance, one orderly man to each car.

EVACUATIONS BY TRANSPORT.

Slightly wounded will be evacuated to ACHEUX by,

(1). Reserve Motor Ambulances.
(2). Horse Ambulances.
(3). Fitted G.S. Wagons.

ROADS.

The road north and south from COIRNEUX to BUS, and thence to ACHEUX has been set aside for Horse Transport moving slightly wounded cases to the Corps Collecting Station at ACHEUX. Motor Ambulances can also use this road for this purpose. This road can be used in both directions.

Within the Town of BUS (J.26.C.24) from the situation of the Main Dressing Station 94th. Field Ambulance to approximately T.26.a.31 the road corner north west of the town. Ambulance transport pass both ways.

RATIONS.

Necessary instructions have been issued to the QUARTERMASTER.

Lieut-Colonel, R.A.M.C.
Commanding,
95th Field Ambulance,
31st Division

Confidential 31st Division Vol VII

War Diary
of
63rd Field Amb.

1st July to 31st July
1916

WAR DIARY

INTELLIGENCE SUMMARY

Army Form C. 2118.

July 19 15
95th Field Ambulance (1)

Place	Date	Hour	Summary of Events and Information	Remarks and references to Appendices
BUS-LES-ARTOIS	1/7/16		95th Field Ambulance, 31st Division (LE MAB FRANCE) The whole unit was taking part in active operations. 57 D NE 1/20,000. Tent subdivisions were at Main Dressing Station. A Section – Capt G Mitchell – BUS B " – Lieut A G Winter – BUS C " – Capt W Hunt – WARENMONT WOOD (Reserve Main Dressing Station) Bearer Subdivisions Under Capt C M WEST and GS by Lieut L M INGLE at Adv. Dressing Station at EUSTON. Wounded were there collected from 93rd Bde. 31st Div. & evacuated. No sick. Lieut J V DUFFY transferred to this unit from R.E. 29th Div. Lieut L M INGLE admitted to 94. F.A. wounded. 6 six burials of the ambulance were wounded. Lieut H B STACKPOOLE arrived from No 5 General Hospital ROUEN for duty.	

WAR DIARY

INTELLIGENCE SUMMARY.

95th F.A. July 1916. Army Form C. 2118. (2)

Place	Date	Hour	Summary of Events and Information	Remarks and references to Appendices
Bus-les Artois	3/7/16		(continues) Lieut R.L. BLENKHORN Jones for duty from No 6 General Hospital ROUEN. A & B (Stretcher Bearers) Sections returned to BUS from A.D.S. Dressing Station. 4 A Section moved on to WARNIMONT WOOD. Total Casualties evacuated in 3 days of operations Officers - Nil - O.R. lying 695 - sitting 345 - wounded 125 - deaths 3. Total 1165.	
-Do-	4/7/16		B section stretcher bearers moved to WARNIMONT WOOD, the remainder of unit also proceeded there	
WARNIMONT WOOD	5/7/16		A & B sections moved from WARNIMONT WOOD to BEAUVAL.	
BERNAVILLE	6/7/16		O Sect. Stretcher Bearers left A.D.S. at EUSTON, arrives WARNIMONT WOOD A & B Sects. moved from BEAUVAL to BERNAVILLE.	

Army Form C. 2118.

WAR DIARY
INTELLIGENCE SUMMARY.

9/5 F.A. July 1916 (3)

(Erase heading not required.)

Instructions regarding War Diaries and Intelligence Summaries are contained in F.S. Regs., Part II. and the Staff Manual respectively. Title pages will be prepared in manuscript.

Place	Date	Hour	Summary of Events and Information	Remarks and references to Appendices
BERNAVILLE	7/7/16		C Section left WARNIMONT WOOD and arrives at BERNAVILLE.	
-Do-	8/7/16		No 60316 Acting Sergt Major HOOPER, F.W.H. 68824 Pte MACK, W. & 68862 Pte PLAIN J.S. transferred to No 4 C.C.S. sick. No 59489 Q.M.S. GWYNN, C.G. reinstated to permanent rank of Sergt Major with effect from 27/6/16. Auxly. R.A.M. Corps orders No 24, dated 27/6/16. Unit moves to AUXI-LE CHATEAU. Unit entrains at AUXI-LE CHATEAU for THIENNES, from thence marches to ROBECQ.	
ROBECQ	9/7/16			
-Do-	11/7/16		Lieut & Q.M. G.E.TOWN transfers sick to 2nd London C.C.S. No 68829 Capt. MATTHEWS reverts to rank of private at his own request.	
-Do-	17/7/16		Lieut J. DUFFY to 2nd London CCS sick. also 2 men to No. 7 CCS R.A.M.S. XI Corps inspects the Camp. 2 officers (Capt. G MITCHELL & Lieut H.B. STACKPOOLE) 2 N.Cos, 72 men proceeded to take over H.A.D.S at VIELLE CHAPELLE & LA FLINQUE (36A R 34 A) (36-M 16 b)	

1 AUG 1916
FIELD AMBULANCE
R.A.M.C.

WAR DIARY

INTELLIGENCE SUMMARY

Army Form C. 2118.

95th F.A. July 1916

Place	Date	Hour	Summary of Events and Information	Remarks and references to Appendices
RODECQ	14/7/16		Cont. Form 2/3 South Midlands F.A. under orders of A.D.M.S. 31st Div. 5th 65637 Sgt. BLACKBURN F. to No. 7 C.C.S. sick.	
VIEILLE CHAPELLE	15/7/16		Unit moved to VIEILLE CHAPELLE & took over Dressing Station vacated by 2/3 S.M.F.A. 23 N.C.Os then proceeded to Adv. Dressing Station for duty	
- Do -	17/7/16		Divisional Baths at VIEILLE CHAPELLE & CROIX BARBÉE taken over under orders A.D.M.S. 31st Div. 5th	
- Do -	18/7/16		1 N.C.O. proceeded to A.D.S. for duty	
- Do -	19/7/16		6 Pte. proceeded acting Lce/Cpl. with pay & one Act. Lce. Cpl. without pay.	
- Do -	20/7/16		R. Bus x 1 Cpl. proceeds Main Dressing Station & then A.D.S. at LA FLINQUE. Lt. & hon. G.E. TOWN rejoined, discharged to duty from No. 14 General Hospital BOULOGNE	

95 7 A. July 1916. (5)

WAR DIARY or INTELLIGENCE SUMMARY

Army Form C. 2118.

Place	Date	Hour	Summary of Events and Information	Remarks and references to Appendices
VIEILLE CHAPELLE	24/7/16		A.D.S at LA FLINQUE handed over to 2/3 S.M.F.A. 61st Divsn. A.D.S at ST VAAST - (M 30.c. map 36A) + R.A.P at LA COUTURE (X 5.c. (B 6 a.)) taken over during night 23/24 July under instructions from A.D.M.S. 31st Divsn.	
Do	25/7/16		Baths at RICHEBOURG ST VAAST taken over — Acknowledged from A.D.M.S 31 Divsn. effectn from 27/7/16. No 68889 Sergt. PRIME B.H. promoted acting Q.M.S. without pay with effect from 27/7/16. 1 Cpl 1 Pte proceeded for duty at XI C Corps Rest Station - No 36657 Pte Jackson G.E. transferred to No 7 C.C.S suffering from accidental injury to right eye. 1 Pte reported for duty from 93rd F.A.	
Do	26/7/16		Baths at CROIX BARBÉE handed over to 93rd F.A. in view of A.D.M.S 31st Divsn. Lieut. A.G. WINTER transferred to 2/5 London Cas. Sick.	

96th FIELD AMBULANCE R.A.M.C. 1 AUG 1916

95th F.A.   July 1916.   6

Army Form C. 2118.

WAR DIARY
INTELLIGENCE SUMMARY.
(Erase heading not required.)

Instructions regarding War Diaries and Intelligence Summaries are contained in F. S. Regs., Part II. and the Staff Manual respectively. Title pages will be prepared in manuscript.

Place	Date	Hour	Summary of Events and Information	Remarks and references to Appendices
VIEILLE CHAPELLE	27/7/16		Capt. T.B. NICHOLLS returns to duty from No 4 C.C.S. 2 Corporals promoted at length with pay to complete establishment.	
			1 N.C.O. transferred to No 7 Cas Sect.	
	26/7/16		2 Lance Corpls. promoted Corporals into pay to complete establishment. A.D.M.S. 31st Division inspected men drawing station	
	31/7/16		Surg. Genl. PIKE. C.M.G. D.S.O. DMS FIRST ARMY inspected main Dressing Station	

E. B. Knox
Lieut-Colonel, R.A.M.C.
Commanding,
95th Field Ambulance,
31st Division.

Confidential 31st Divn. Vol. XIII
August 1916

War Diary

95th & 3rd Ambulance

Aug 1916.

COMMITTEE FOR THE
MEDICAL HISTORY OF THE WAR
Date −9 OCT. 1916

SECRET.

WAR DIARY
INTELLIGENCE SUMMARY
(Erase heading not required.)

Army Form C. 2118
31 AUG 1916

Instructions regarding War Diaries and Intelligence Summaries are contained in F. S. Regs. Part II. and the Staff Manual respectively. Title pages will be prepared in manuscript.

95th. FIELD AMBULANCE.   31st. DIVISION.   AUGUST 1916   (1)

Place	Date	Hour	Summary of Events and Information	Remarks and references to Appendices
VIEILLE CHAPELLE	1/8/16		HEADQUARTERS of the Unit is still at VIEILLE CHAPELLE. The MAIN DRESSING STATION being at (R.31.a. map 36.a.) The A.D.S. at ST. VAAST (M.32.c. map 36.a.) A COLLECTING POST at LACOUTURE (x.5.d. map 36.a.), DIVISIONAL BATHS at VIEILLE CHAPELLE and ST. VAAST which are still staffed by the personnel of the Unit.	cK
"	2/8/16		1 N.C.O. and 5 men R.A.M.C. reported for duty as reinforcements from No. 5 BASE.	cK
"	3/8/16		D.M.S. 1st ARMY inspected MAIN DRESSING STATION and A.D.S. at ST. VAAST. Major-General R. WANLESS-O'GOWAN C.B. Commanding 31st Division inspected the Field Ambulance and Camp and BATHS at VIEILLE CHAPELLE.	cK
"	4/8/16		A.D.M.S. 31st Division inspected MAIN DRESSING STATION.	cK
"	5/8/16		D.D.M.S. XI. CORPS inspected MAIN DRESSING STATION	cK
"	6/8/16		A.D.M.S. 31st Division inspected MAIN DRESSING STATION.	cK
"	8/8/16		Lieut A. FINLAY and 2 men reported for duty.	cK
"	10/8/16		3 (M.T.) A.S.C. Drivers reported for duty from 31st Divisional Supply Column.	cK

WAR DIARY
INTELLIGENCE SUMMARY.

(Erase heading not required.)

(2)

Stamp: 98th FIELD AMBULANCE C.2118 — 31 AUG 1916 — R.A.M.C.

Army Form C.2118

Instructions regarding War Diaries and Intelligence Summaries are contained in F.S. Regs., Part II. and the Staff Manual respectively. Title pages will be prepared in manuscript.

Place	Date	Hour	Summary of Events and Information	Remarks and references to Appendices
CHAPELLE VIEILLE	11/8/16		Captain T.L. Nicholls transferred to the 50th. Field Ambulance.	K
"	13/8/16		1 Sergeant R.A.M.C. reported for duty from No.18 Casualty Clearing Station. Lieut H.B.STACPOOLE evacuated to 2nd London Casualty Clearing Station and one private transferred to No. 7 Casualty Clearing Station (Wounded).	K
"	14/8/16		Captain E.U.RUSSELL reported for duty from No. 3 Casualty Clearing Station.	K
"	15/8/16		A.D.M.S. 31st. Division inspected MAIN DRESSING STATION.	K
"	16/8/16		Captain F.A. BELAM reported for duty from West Riding Casualty Clearing Station.	K
"	17/8/16		D.D.M.S. X1 CORPS. inspected MAIN DRESSING STATION.	K
"	21/8/16		R.A.POST at FACTORY POST handed over to Medical Officer 13th. East Yorks., and the R.A.POST at PLUM STREET handed over to Medical Officer 2/7 Worcester Regt. as directed by D.D.M.S. X1 CORPS. Lieut A.E.SUTTON reported for duty from X1 CORPS MOUNTED TROOPS. 1 Private R.A.M.C. transferred to BASE (instructions A.D.S.S. 31st. Division).	K

2353 Wt. W2544/1454 700,000 5/15 D.D.&L. A.D.S.S./Forms/C.2118.

Army Form C2118

WAR DIARY
or
INTELLIGENCE SUMMARY.
(Erase heading not required.)

(3)

Instructions regarding War Diaries and Intelligence Summaries are contained in F. S. Regs., Part II. and the Staff Manual respectively. Title pages will be prepared in manuscript.

Place	Date	Hour	Summary of Events and Information	Remarks and references to Appendices
VIEILLE CHAPELLE	24/8/16		3 Privates R.A.M.C. reported for duty from BASE ROUEN.	eK
"	25/8/16		1 Private R.A.M.C. transferred to No. 7 Casualty Clearing Station (Sick)	eK
"	27/8/16		D.A.D.M.S. 31st. Division inspected ADVANCED DRESSING STATION. Lieut H. YOUNG granted 14 days Special Leave on termination of his first years contract.	eK
"	28/8/16		A.D.M.S. 31st. Division inspected MAIN DRESSING STATION.	eK
"	29/8/16		2 A.S.C. Drivers reported for duty from 31st. Divisional Train.	eK

C. Kerr
Lieut-Colonel, R.A.M.C.
Commanding,
95th Field Ambulance,
31st Division.

Army Form W.3091.

Cover for Documents.

11. MEDICAL CASES - SPECIAL CASES. (C)

Nature of Enclosures.

GLANDERS.

Notes, or Letters written.

Army Form C. 2118.

95th Field Amb[?]

WAR DIARY
INTELLIGENCE SUMMARY

SEPTEMBER 1916. (1)

(Erase heading not required.)

Instructions regarding War Diaries and Intelligence Summaries are contained in F. S. Regs., Part II. and the Staff Manual respectively. Title pages will be prepared in manuscript.

Place	Date	Hour	Summary of Events and Information	Remarks and references to Appendices
VIEILLE CHAPELLE	1/9/16		25th. FIELD AMBULANCE. 31st. DIVISION. HEADQUARTERS of the UNIT is still at VIEILLE CHAPELLE. The MAIN DRESSING STATION being at (R.34. a. Map 36. a.) The A.D.S. at St. VAAST (M.32. c. Map 36. a.). A COLLECTING POST at LA COUTURE (M.5.d. Map 36. a.). DIVISIONAL BATHS at VIEILLE CHAPELLE and St. VAAST which are still staffed by the personnel of the unit.	
"	5/9/16		1 man R.A.M.C. transferred to S.O. Cavalry Base for disposal. (under age). D.M.S. 1st. Army and A.D.M.S. 31st. Division inspected MAIN DRESSING STATION, A.D.S and COLLECTING POST at LA COUTURE.	
"	8/9/16		1 N.C.O. R.A.M.C. evacuated to No. 7 C.C.S. (sick). 2 men R.A.M.C. reported for duty from No.5 BASE ROUEN.	
"	9/9/16		2 N.C.O's and 1 man R.A.M.C. transferred to C.C.S. (sick).	
"	10/9/16		3 men R.A.M.C. transferred to C.C.S. (sick).	
"	11/9/16		Captain G. Mitchell, R.A.M.C. transferred to 1/2 London C.C.S. also 1 man R.A.M.C. (sick)	

Army Form C. 2118.

WAR DIARY

INTELLIGENCE SUMMARY

(Erase heading not required.)

95th Field Ambce

Instructions regarding War Diaries and Intelligence Summaries are contained in F. S. Regs. Part II. and the Staff Manual respectively. Title pages will be prepared in manuscript.

Place	Date	Hour	Summary of Events and Information	Remarks and references to Appendices
VIEILLE CHAPELLE	12/9/16.		D.A.D.M.S. XI Corps SANITARY SECTION inspected MAIN DRESSING STATION.	
"	13/9/16.		Lieut. H. Young, R.A.M.C. reported for duty from Special leave to Scotland.	
"	13/9/16.		A.D.M.S. 31st Division inspected MAIN DRESSING STATION, A.D.S. and COLLECTING POST at LA COUTURE.	
"	14/9/16.		C.E. XI Corps and C.R.E. 31st Division inspected MAIN DRESSING STATION.	
"	16/9/16.		Lieut. A. FINLAY R.A.M.C. transferred for duty to 254 TUNNELLING COMPANY ROYAL ENGINEERS. (Authority D.D.M.S. XI Corps No. C/283 dated 16-9-16).	
			Capt. I. Campbell, R.A.M.C. reported for duty from 94th Field Ambulance.	
"	17/9/16.		MAIN DRESSING STATION at ZELOBES (M.27. C.O.5) was taken over from 93rd Field Ambulance in accordance with instructions from A.D.M.S. 31st Division. (Authority R.A.M.C. Operation Order No. 4 by COLONEL A.W. BEWLEY, A.D.M.S. 31st Division dated 15-9-16.)	
			BATHS at CROIX BAREE (M.28. d.) taken over from 93rd Field Ambulance (Authority A.D.M.S. 31st Division M/3494 dated 16-9-16.)	

Army Form C. 2118.

WAR DIARY
INTELLIGENCE SUMMARY

(Erase heading not required.)

Instructions regarding War Diaries and Intelligence Summaries are contained in F.S. Regs., Part II. and the Staff Manual respectively. Title pages will be prepared in manuscript.

(3) 95th Field Ambulance

Place	Date	Hour	Summary of Events and Information	Remarks and references to Appendices
VIEILLE CHAPELLE	19/9/16.		COLONEL SULLIVAN 31st Division and Staff inspected MAIN DRESSING STATION and A.D.S.	
			Lieut. & Quartermaster G.E. TOWN, R.A.M.C. proceeded to ENGLAND under orders (Authority M.S. G.H.Q. No. 17643 dated 10-9-16.)	
			Captain W. HUNT proceeded on Special Leave to IRELAND.	E.B.S.
"	23/9/16.		1 Private proceeded for 10 days leave to ENGLAND.	E.B.S.
"	25/9/16.		Lieut. & Quartermaster C.E.T. RICHMOND reported for duty from No. 5 Cavalry Field Ambulance.	E.B.S.
"	26/9/16.		1 Sergeant transferred to 94th Field Ambulance for duty, and 1 Sergeant reported for duty from 16 Casualty Clearing Station.	E.B.S.
"	27/9/16.		Capt. W. HUNT returned from Special Leave to Ireland.	E.B.S.
"	30/9/16.		Brigadier General E.P. LAMBERT, C.B. and A.D.M.S. 31st. Division inspected M.D.S.	
			Capt. E.E. RUSSELL transferred to A.D.M.S. 33nd. Division for duty.	E.B.S.
			Capt. I. CAMPBELL transferred to 1/2 London Casualty Clearing Station. Sick.	
			1 N.C.O. proceeded to England on 10 days leave.	E.B.S.

E.B.S.
Lieut-Colonel, R.A.M.C.
Commanding,
95th Field Ambulance,
31st Division.

Confidential

Volume X

War Diary.

95th Field Ambulance 31st Division

October 1916.

SECRET.

95/4/4

Army Form C. 2118

WAR DIARY
INTELLIGENCE SUMMARY
OCTOBER, 1916.

(Erase heading not required.)

Instructions regarding War Diaries and Intelligence Summaries are contained in F.S. Regs., Part II. and the Staff Manual respectively. Title Pages will be prepared in manuscript.

Place	Date	Hour	Summary of Events and Information	Remarks and references to Appendices
VIEILLE CHAPELLE.	1/10/16.		**95th FIELD AMBULANCE, 31st. DIVISION.** HEADQUARTERS of the Unit is still at VIEILLE CHAPELLE. The MAIN DRESSING STATIONS being at (R 34.a., Map 36 a) and (R 27 e Map 36A). The ADVANCED DRESSING STATION at St. VAAST (M.32.c Map 36A.) A Collecting Post at LACOUTURE (X5 d Map 36A.) Divisional Baths at VIEILLE CHAPELLE St. VAAST and CROIXBARBEE which are still staffed by the personnel of this Unit. Captain G.W. ANDERSON, R.A.M.C., Lieut. J.F.C. O'Meara, R.A.M.C. and Lieut. D.T. SKEEN, R.A.M.C. reported for duty from 2nd./3rd. South Midland Field Ambulance.	ck ck ck ck
"	2/10/16		Lieut. R. BURGES, R.A.M.C. proceeded on 14 days Special Leave to England.	ck
"	3/10/16		1 Private R.A.M.C. proceeded to England on 10days Special Leave.	ck
"	4/10/16		MAIN DRESSING STATION at VIEILLE CHAPELLE (R 34 a. Map 36 A) ADVANCED DRESSING STATION at St. VAAST (M.32 c. Map 36A) A Collecting Post at La COUTURE (X5 d Map 36 A). The Baths at VIEILLE CHAPELLE St. VAAST and CROIXBARBEE were handed over to the 15th Field Ambulance 5th Division. 16 M.T., A.S.C. Drivers, 5 Siddeley Deasy Ambulance Cars, 2 Ford Ambulance Cars and 2 Motor Cycles were handed over to the 15 th Field Ambulance 5th Division.	ck

Army Form C. 2118

95th. F.a.

WAR DIARY

INTELLIGENCE SUMMARY

2.

(Erase heading not required.)

Instructions regarding War Diaries and Intelligence Summaries are contained in F.S. Regs., Part II. and the Staff Manual respectively. Title Pages will be prepared in manuscript.

Place	Date	Hour	Summary of Events and Information	Remarks and references to Appendices
ZELOBES.	4/10/16.		The Unit moved to ZELOBES (R 27 c Map 36 A).	
"	5/10/16.		Lieut. J.N. DEACON, R.A.M.C. reported for duty from 2nd./4th. Royal Berkshire Regiment.	
			Lieut. J. O'MEARA R.A.M.C. transferred to A.D.M.S. 61st. Division for duty.	
			MAIN DRESSING STATION at ZELOBES (R 27 c Map 36 A) handed over to the 15th Field Ambulance, 5th Division.	
CALONNE.	5/10/16.		The Unit moved to CALONNE (Q. 8. b. Map 36 A)	
"	7/10/16.		3 Privates R.A.M.C. reported for duty as reinforcements.	
"			1 A.S.C. Driver reported for duty from the 31st Divisional Train.	
"	8/10/16.		The Unit moved to MERVILLE (K. 29. Map 36 A) to entrain for CANDAS. Unit entrained at Midnight.	
VEAUCHELLES.	9/10/16.		Arrived at CANDAS 12 noon and proceeded by road to VEAUCHELLES (I 33. a. Map 57 D)	
"	10/10/16.		Lieut. J.N. DEACON, R.A.M.C. transferred to 10th East Yorks. for duty.	

WAR DIARY
INTELLIGENCE SUMMARY
(Erase heading not required.)

Army Form C. 2118

Place	Date	Hour	Summary of Events and Information	Remarks and references to Appendices
VAUCHELLES	10/10/16.		**COMPLIMENTARY.** "Sir D. HAIG, Commander in Chief of the British Expeditionary force in FRANCE expressed his high appreciation in the soldierly way the Unit marched passed him at BEAUQUESNE on the 19th instant, and directed that all officers N.C.O's and men should be so informed."	C.A.
"	11/10/16.		1 N.C.O. R.A.M.C. proceeded to England on 10 days Special Leave.	C.A.
"	13/10/16.		3 Privates transferred to the 42nd Heavy Artillery Group for duty and are struck off the strength accordingly.	C.A.
"	14/10/16.		1 N.C.O. transferred to No. 44 Casualty Clearing Station sick.	C.A.
"	15/10/16.		Captain D.T. SKEEn, R.A.M.C., proceeded to No. 4 Casualty Clearing Station for temporary duty.	C.A.
"	15/10/16.		1 N.C.O. and 1 Private (M.T., A.S.C.) and 2 Motor Cycles transferred to from No. 77 Company A.S.C. for duty.	C.A.
"	17/10/16.		1 Private transferred to 93rd Field Ambulance, sick.	C.A.
COIGNEUX.	17/10/16.		The Unit moved to COIGNEUX (J. 9 central Map 57 D).	C.A.

Army Form C. 2118

WAR DIARY
INTELLIGENCE SUMMARY
(Erase heading not required.)

Instructions regarding War Diaries and Intelligence Summaries are contained in F.S. Regs., Part II. and the Staff Manual respectively. Title Pages will be prepared in manuscript.

Place	Date	Hour	Summary of Events and Information	Remarks and references to Appendices
COIGNEUX.	17/10/16.		A Holding Party of 1 officer and 7 other ranks (strength 1 officer and 7 other ranks) took over MAIN DRESSING STATION at COIGNEUX (16/10/16.	
			1 Bearer Sub-division took over ADVANCED DRESSING STATION at HEBUTERNE (K.15 b. 6 2 Map 57 D)	
			1 Bearer Sub-division took over the ADVANCED DRESSING STATION at COLINCAMPS (K 35. c 06. Map 57 D).	
			A Holding Party of 1 N.C.O. and 6 men took over the Field Ambulance MAIN DRESSING STATIONS at BUS-LES-ARTOIS (J. 26. Map 57 D), and WARNIMONT WOOD (I. 24. d. Map 57D)	
"	17/10/16.		ADVANCED DRESSING STATION at COLINCAMPS handed over to a Field Ambulance of the 3rd Division.	
			MAIN DRESSING STATION at BUS handed over to a Field Ambulance of the 3rd Division.	
"	18/10/16.		A.D.M.S. 31st. Division inspected the Camp.	
"	19/10/16.		1 Private R.A.M.C., and 1 Driver A.S.C., discharged C.C.S. for duty.	
"	23/10/16.		1 A.S.C. Driver proceeded to England on 10 days Special Leave.	
"	24/10/16.		MAIN DRESSING STATION AT WARNIMONT WOOD handed over to 93rd Field Ambulance.	

1875 Wt. W593/826 1,000,000 4/15 J.B.C. & A. A.D.S.S./Forms/C.2118.

WAR DIARY

Army Form C. 2118

Place	Date	Hour	Summary of Events and Information	Remarks and references to Appendices
COIGNEUX	24/10/16.		Captain T. MILLING transferred from 93rd Field Ambulance for duty.	
"	25/10/16.		1 A.S.C., N.C.O., proceeded to ENGLAND on 10 days Special Leave.	
			1 R.A.M.C. Private evacuated to 94th Field Ambulance, wounded.	
"	26/10/16.		2 R.A.M.C. Privates reported for duty as reinforcements from Base Details, ROUEN.	
			Major-General R. Wanless O'GOWAN, C.B., inspected the Camp.	
"	30/10/16.		D.D.M.S. 13th Corps and A.D.M.S. 31st. Division inspected the Camp.	

Lieut-Colonel, R.A.M.C.
Commanding,
95th Field Ambulance,
31st Division.

140/862

Volume XI

Vol 9

Confidential

S/

War Diary

95th Field Ambulance

31st Division

November 1916.

COMMITTEE FOR THE
MEDICAL HISTORY OF THE WAR
Date -3 JAN. 1917

SECRET

Army Form C. 2118

Instructions regarding War Diaries and Intelligence Summaries are contained in F.S. Regs., Part II. and the Staff Manual respectively. Title Pages will be prepared in manuscript.

WAR DIARY

INTELLIGENCE SUMMARY

NOVEMBER.

(Erase heading not required.)

Place	Date	Hour	Summary of Events and Information	Remarks and references to Appendices
COIGNEUX.	1/11/16		The HEADQUARTERS of the Unit is still at COIGNEUX. The MAIN DRESSING STATION being at (J.9.central Map 57 D). The ADVANCED DRESSING STATION at HEBUTERNE (K.15.b. Map 57 D) D.A.D.M.S. XIIIth Corps inspected the ADVANCED DRESSING STATION.	
"	2/11/16.		No. 63512 Staff-Sergeant J. HARVEY, R.A.M.C. evacuated to CASUALTY CLEARING STATION wounded at HEBUTERNE (died on 3-11-16).	
"	9/11/16		The D.D.M.S. XIIIth Corps inspected the MAIN DRESSING STATION.	
"	10/11/16		The G.O.C., 31st. Division inspected the MAIN DRESSING STATION.	
"	11/11/16		No. 68622 Private R. EARNSHAW, R.A.M.C. was killed by a Shell at HEBUTERNE.	
"	13/11/16		The whole Unit took part in Active Operations in the HEBUTERNE Sector. Two Tent Sub-Divisions were employed at COIGNEUX and one at the ADVANCED DRESSING STATION, HEBUTERNE. Two Bearer SubDivisions were employed at the ADVANCED DRESSING STATION HEBUTERNE and 1 Officer and 38 Other Ranks with 18 stretchers at the Collecting Post in HOME AVENUE (K.21.c.3.2.) Wounded were collected from the 92nd Infantry Brigade area and evacuated. Totals being Officers 15, Other Ranks 247. J.B.C. & A. A.D.S.S.	

WAR DIARY or INTELLIGENCE SUMMARY

Army Form C. 2118

Place	Date	Hour	Summary of Events and Information	Remarks and references to Appendices
COIGNEUX.	13/11/16		The D.D.M.S. XIIIth Corps and the A.D.M.S. 31st Division inspected the MAIN DRESSING STATION.	
"	14/11/16		The G.O.C. 31st Division inspected the MAIN DRESSING STATION.	
"	22/11/16		Lieutenant T.G. FENTON, R.A.M.C., reported for duty from Cambridge Hospital, ALDERSHOT.	
"	24/11/16		Captain D.T. SKEEN, R.A.M.C., reported for duty from No. 4 C.C.S.	
"			Captain D.T. SKEEN, R.A.M.C. took over charge 13th York & Lancs.	
"	25/11/16		D.D.M.S. and D.A.D.M.S. of the XIIIth Corps inspected the MAIN DRESSING STATION.	
"			Captain W. HUNT, R.A.M.C. was awarded the Military Cross for gallantry at HEBUTERNE.	
"	27/11/16		Captain G.W. ANDERSON, R.A.M.C. took over temporary Medical Charge of 11th East Yorks	
"			Captain J. CONNELL, R.A.M.C. reported for duty from 93rd Field Ambulance.	

Lieut-Colonel, R.A.M.C.
Commanding,
95th Field Ambulance,
31st Division.

Confidential

Volume XII.

140/603

Vol 10

War Diary

95th Field Ambulance

31st Division.

December 1916.

WAR DIARY
or
INTELLIGENCE SUMMARY

(Erase heading not required.)

Army Form C. 2118

DECEMBER

Place	Date	Hour	Summary of Events and Information	Remarks and references to Appendices
COIGNEUX.	1/12/16.		The HEADQUARTERS of the Unit is still at COIGNEUX. The MAIN DRESSING STATION being at (J.9.central Map 57 D). The ADVANCED DRESSING STATION at HEBUTERNE (K.15.b. Map 57 D).	
"	3/12/16.		D.D.M.S. and D.A.D.M.S. XIIIth Corps inspected the MAIN DRESSING STATION. A.D.M.S. inspected the MAIN DRESSING STATION.	
"	6/12/16.		The ADVANCED DRESSING STATION at HEBUTERNE (K.15.b. Map 57 D) was handed over to the 93rd Field Ambulance. D.A.D.M.S. XIIIth Corps inspected the MAIN DRESSING STATION.	
"	9/12/16.		Captain F.A. BELAM, R.A.M.C. proceeded to take over Temporary Medical Charge of the 13th East Yorkshire Regiment.	
"	11/12/16.		Captain G.W. Anderson, R.A.M.C. reported for duty from the 11th East Yorkshire Regiment.	
"	15/12/16.		Lieutenant T.G. FENTON, R.A.M.C. proceeded to take over Temporary Medical Charge of the 12th K.O.Y.L.I. Capt. G.W. ANDERSON, F.A.M.C. proceeded to take over Temporary Medical Charge of the	

Army Form C. 2118.

WAR DIARY
or
INTELLIGENCE SUMMARY.
(Erase heading not required.)

-2-

Place	Date	Hour	Summary of Events and Information	Remarks and references to Appendices
COIGNEUX	17/12/16.		12th Battalion York & Lancs. Regiment.	
"	20/12/16.		A.D.M.S. inspected the MAIN DRESSING STATION.	
"	23/12/16.		Lieut-Colonel E. B. KNOX, R.A.M.C. proceeded on 10 days Special Leave to ENGLAND.	
"	25/12/16		Lieutenant T. G. FENTON, R.A.M.C., returned from temporary duty with 12th K.O.Y.L.I	
"	25/12/16		A.D.M.S., 31st Division addressed and inspected the UNIT.	
"			MAJOR-GENERAL R. WANLESS O'GOWAN, C.B., addressed and inspected the UNIT.	
"	28/12/16.		D.A.D.M.S., 31st Division inspected the MAIN DRESSING STATION.	
"	30/12/16.		Lieut-Colonel E. B. KNOX, R.A.M.C., returned from 10 days Special Leave to ENGLAND.	

EBKnox
Lieut-Colonel, R.A.M.C.
Commanding,
95th Field Ambulance,
31st Division.

Instructions regarding War Diaries and Intelligence Summaries are contained in F. S. Regs., Part II. and the Staff Manual respectively. Title pages will be prepared in manuscript.

"Confidential."

Volume XIII.

31 / 140/1943

Vol XI

War Diary.

95th Field Ambulance, 31st Division

January 1917.

COMMITTEE FOR THE
MEDICAL HISTORY OF THE WAR
Date 13 MAR. 1917

SECRET

Army Form C. 2118

WAR DIARY
INTELLIGENCE SUMMARY

JANUARY 1917.

(Erase heading not required.)

Instructions regarding War Diaries and Intelligence Summaries are contained in F. S. Regs., Part II. and the Staff Manual respectively. Title Pages will be prepared in manuscript.

Place	Date	Hour	Summary of Events and Information	Remarks and references to Appendices
COIGNEUX.	1-1-17.		The HEADQUARTERS of the UNIT at COIGNEUX. The MAIN DRESSING STATION being at (Map 57 D. J.9.central.)	
			Captain R. BURGES, R.A.M.C., took over Temporary Medical Charge of 15th East Yorks.	
			Captain H. YOUNG, R.A.M.C., took over Temporary Medical Charge of 10th East Yorks.	
			Captain G.W. ANDERSON, R.A.M.C., reported from duty with 15th York & Lancs.	
"	3-1-17.		D.A.D.M.S. Sanitary Fifth Army inspected the MAIN DRESSING STATION.	
"	4-1-17.		D.M.S., Fifth Army, A.D.M.S., 31st Division, inspected the MAIN DRESSING STATION.	
"	5-1-17.		3 N.C.O's., R.A.M.C., attended ANTI-GAS SCHOOL for course of instruction in ANTI-GAS precaution.	
"	7-1-17.		D.A.D.M.S., XIIIth Corps and A.D.M.S., 31st Division, inspected the MAIN DRESSING STATION.	
"	10-1-17.		The MAIN DRESSING STATION at (Map 57 D J.9.central.) was handed to 57th Field Ambulance.	

A.D.S.S./Forms/C. 2118.

Army Form C. 2118

WAR DIARY

~~INTELLIGENCE SUMMARY~~

(Erase heading not required.)

Instructions regarding War Diaries and Intelligence Summaries are contained in F.S. Regs., Part II. and the Staff Manual respectively. Title Pages will be prepared in manuscript.

Place	Date	Hour	Summary of Events and Information	Remarks and references to Appendices
BEAUVAL.	10-1-17.		The UNIT proceeded to BEAUVAL and took over XIIIth CORPS REST STATION at G.16.D.8.8.	CM
"	13-1-17.		Captain R. BURGES, R.A.M.C., reported for duty from 12th East Yorks.	CM
"	14-1-17.		A.D.M.S., 31st Division inspected the CORPS REST STATION.	CM
"	16-1-17.		No. 68605 Sgt. BROWN, F., R.A.M.C., proceeded to ENGLAND (Candidate for Commission) (Authority 31st Division 1786 A dated 6-1-17.)	CM
"	19-1-17.		A.D.M.S., 31st Division inspected CORPS REST STATION.	CM
"	21-1-17.		D.A.D.M.S.,(Sanitary)Fifth Army inspected CORPS REST STATION.	CM
"	22-1-17.		D.D.M.S., XIIIth Corps and A.D.M.S., 31st Division inspected the CORPS REST STATION.	CM
"	24-1-17.		D.D.M.S., XIIIth Corps inspected the CORPS REST STATION.	CM
"	27-1-17.		A.D.M.S., 31st Division, inspected the CORPS REST STATION.	CM

Army Form C. 2118.

WAR DIARY

(Erase heading not required.)

Place	Date	Hour	Summary of Events and Information	Remarks and references to Appendices
BEAUVAL.	29-1-17.		D.M.S. XIIIth Corps and A.D.M.S., 31st Division inspected the CORPS REST STATION.	
"	31-1-17.		A.D.M.S., 31st Division inspected the CORPS REST STATION.	

95TH FIELD AMBULANCE.
1 FEB 1917

C.W. Knott
Lieut-Colonel, R.A.M.C.
Commanding,
95th Field Ambulance,
31st Division.

Confidential

140/991

Volume XIV

Vol 1"

War Diary.

95th Field Ambulance 31st Division

February 1917.

COMMITTEE FOR THE
MEDICAL HISTORY OF THE WAR
Date 4— APR. 1917

Army Form C. 2118.

WAR DIARY

~~INTELLIGENCE SUMMARY~~

(Erase heading not required.)

FEBRUARY 1917.

Instructions regarding War Diaries and Intelligence Summaries are contained in F. S. Regs., Part II. and the Staff Manual respectively. Title pages will be prepared in manuscript.

Place	Date	Hour	Summary of Events and Information	Remarks and references to Appendices
BEAUVAL.	1-2-17.		The HEADQUARTERS of the Unit at BEAUVAL. XIII Corps Rest Station. Map Reference G.16.d.8.8.	CM
"	2-2-17.		A.D.M.S. 31st Division inspected the CORPS REST STATION.	CM
"	8-2-17.		D.D.M.S., XIII Corps inspected the CORPS REST STATION.	CM
"	8-2-17.		D.A.D.M.S., 31st Division, inspected the CORPS REST STATION.	CM
"	10-2-17.		D.A.D.M.S., 31st Division, inspected the CORPS REST STATION.	CM
"			An outbreak of Fire occurred in one of the patients Marquees.	CM
"	11-2-17.		Captain F.A.BELAM, R.A.M.C., took over ~~~~ Medical Charge of 15th West Yorks. Regt.	CM
"	16-2-17.		A Court of Enquiry assembled to investigate the cause of Fire in the patients Marquee	CM
"	17-2-17.		Surgeon-General, W.G.MACPHERSON, inspected the CORPS REST STATION.	CM
"	18-2-17.		Lieut. & Qr.Mr. C.E.T.RICHMOND, R.A.M.C., transferred for duty to No.13 General Hospital, BOULOGNE.	CM

Army Form C. 2118.

WAR DIARY
or
INTELLIGENCE SUMMARY

-2-

(Erase heading not required.)

Instructions regarding War Diaries and Intelligence
Summaries are contained in F. S. Regs., Part II.
and the Staff Manual respectively. Title pages
will be prepared in manuscript.

Place	Date	Hour	Summary of Events and Information	Remarks and references to Appendices
BEAUVAL.	20-2-17.		The CORPS REST STATION at (Map 57 D.G.16.d.8.8.) was handed over to 33rd Field Ambulance. The UNIT proceeded from BEAUVAL to COIGNEUX. (Map reference 57 D J.9.central.)	CM
COIGNEUX.	21-2-17.		UNIT took over MAIN DRESSING STATION at J.9.central.	CM
"	22-2-17.		D.A.D.M.S., 31st Division, inspected the MAIN DRESSING STATION.	CM
			Captain A.E. SUTTON, M.C., R.A.M.C., took over temporary Medical Charge of 15th West Yorks.	CM
"	26-2-17.		Lieut. & Qr.Mr. W. WILSON, R.A.M.C., reported for duty from No.13 General Hospital BOULOGNE.	CM
"	27-2-17.		Court of Enquiry re-assembled at MAIN DRESSING STATION (Map 57D J.9.central) to further investigate the cause of fire at XIII CORPS REST STATION. (Map reference 57D G.16.8.8.8	CM
"	27-2-17.		One N.C.O. and 16 men reported for duty to 10th West Yorks. Regiment at ADVANCED DRESSING STATION, HEBUTERNE, South. (Map 57D K.18.0.5.)	CM
			One Bearer-sub Division with one Officer reported to ADVANCED DRESSING STATION, HEBUTERNE, North.	CM

Army Form C. 2118.

WAR DIARY
or
INTELLIGENCE SUMMARY

(Erase heading not required.)

Place	Date	Hour	Summary of Events and Information	Remarks and references to Appendices
COIGNEUX.	28-3-17.		Lieut. T.G.FENTON, R.A.M.C., reported to 11th East Yorks., for Temporary Medical Duty.	

C. W. Kenny
Lieut-Colonel, R.A.M.C.
Commanding,
95th Field Ambulance,
31st Division.

95TH FIELD AMBULANCE.
MAR 1917

Confidential. 140/2042. Volume XV.

WO/13

War Diary.

95th Field Ambulance. 31st Division

March 1917.

COMMITTEE FOR THE
MEDICAL HISTORY OF THE WAR
Date 11 MAY 1917

Army Form C. 2118.

2/1st Field Ambulance

WAR DIARY

INTELLIGENCE SUMMARY

(Erase heading not required.)

MARCH 1917.

Instructions regarding War Diaries and Intelligence Summaries are contained in F. S. Regs., Part II. and the Staff Manual respectively. Title pages will be prepared in manuscript.

Place	Date	Hour	Summary of Events and Information	Remarks and references to Appendices
COIGNEUX	1-3-17.		HEADQUARTERS of the UNIT at MAIN DRESSING STATION COIGNEUX. Map reference J.9.central. D.A.D.M.S., 31st Division inspected the MAIN DRESSING STATION. One Tent Sub-Division proceeded to No.4 C.C.S., VARENNES for duty.	EK
"	2-3-17.		ADVANCED DRESSING STATION at HEBUTERNE Map reference K.15.b. was taken over from the 93rd Field Ambulance.	EK
"	3-3-17.		AID POST at SAILLY DELL was taken over from the 93rd Field Ambulance.	EK
"	7-3-17.		Capt., W. HUNT, M.C., R.A.M.C., took over temporary Medical Charge of 18th West Yorks.	EK
"	8-3-17.		Lieut. T.G. FENTON, R.A.M.C., reported for duty from the 11th East Yorks.	EK
"	9-3-17.		Lieut. T.G. FENTON, R.A.M.C., took over temporary Medical Charge of 18th West Yorks. vice Capt. W. HUNT, M.C., R.A.M.C., who reported for duty from this unit.	EK
"	10-3-17.		D.D.M.S., Fifth Corps, A.D.M.S., 46th Division inspected the MAIN DRESSING STATION.	EK
"	13-3-17.		MAIN DRESSING STATION at J.9.central, ADVANCED DRESSING STATION at K.15.b. and AID POST at SAILLY DELL were handed over to 1/1st North Midland Field Ambulance. The Unit proceeded to LOUVENCOURT.	EK

9⁶ᵗʰ Field Ambulance

Army Form C. 2118.

WAR DIARY

INTELLIGENCE SUMMARY.

(Erase heading not required.)

-2-

Place	Date	Hour	Summary of Events and Information	Remarks and references to Appendices
LOUVENCOURT.	18-3-17.		The Unit proceeded from LOUVENCOURT to SARTON. Capt. J.S. ALEXANDER, R.A.M.C., reported for duty from the 94th Field Ambulance.	✓
SARTON.	19-3-17.		The Unit proceeded from SARTON to FIENVILLERS. Capt. J.S. ALEXANDER, R.A.M.C., took over Medical Charge of 18th West Yorks, vice Lieut. T.G. FENTON, R.A.M.C., who reported for duty from this Unit.	✓
FIENVILLERS.	20-3-17.		The Unit proceeded from FIENVILLERS to NEUVILLETTE.	✓
NEUVILLETTE.	21-3-17.		The Unit proceeded from NEUVILLETTE to PT. HOUVIN.	✓
PT. HOUVIN.	22-3-17.		The Unit proceeded from PT. HOUVIN to MAREST.	✓
MAREST.	24-3-17.		The Unit proceeded from MAREST to FONTAINE-lez-HERMANS.	✓
FONTAINE-lez-HERMANS.	25-3-17.		The Unit proceeded from FONTAINE-lez-HERMANS, to HOSPITAL HOSPICE, BETHUNE, Map reference 36A (Combined Sheet Bethune) E.11.a. A.D.M.S. 31st Division inspected the Field Ambulance	✓
BETHUNE.	28-3-17.		Capt. H.R. DAVIES, R.A.M.C., reported for duty through the A.D.M.S., 31st Division	✓
"	29-3-17.		Capt. J.G. LEE, R.A.M.C., reported for duty through the A.D.M.S. 31st Division. D.A.D.M.S. XIth Corps inspected the Hospital.	✓

96th Field Ambulance

Army Form C. 2118.

WAR DIARY
INTELLIGENCE SUMMARY

(Erase heading not required.)

Place	Date	Hour	Summary of Events and Information	Remarks and references to Appendices
BETHUNE.	30-3-17.		Capt. J.G. LEE, R.A.M.C., took over Medical Charge of the 15th West Yorks, vice Capt. A.E. SUTTON, R.A.M.C., who reported for duty from this Unit. D.A.D.M.S., 31st Division inspected the Hospital.	

Confidential

Volume XVI
Vol 14

War Diary

95th Field Ambulance. 31st Division

April 1917.

COMMITTEE FOR THE
MEDICAL HISTORY OF THE WAR
Date 6 JUN. 1917

Army Form C. 2118

WAR DIARY
INTELLIGENCE SUMMARY
(Erase heading not required.)

APRIL 1917

95TH FIELD AMBULANCE.

Place	Date	Hour	Summary of Events and Information	Remarks and references to Appendices
BETHUNE.	1-4-17.		HEADQUARTERS OF the UNIT at HOSPITAL-HOSPICE, BETHUNE. Bethune Combine Sheet E.11.b.	
"	2-4-17.		A.D.M.S., 31st Division, inspected the Ambulance.	
"	4-4-17.		Bde.-Gen. INGLES, D.S.O. Commanding 93rd Infantry Brigade, inspected the Transport of the UNIT.	
"	6-4-17.		D.D.M.S., XIIIth Corps, inspected the Ambulance.	
"	8-4-17.		D.D.M.S., XIIIth Corps, inspected the Ambulance.	
"	10-4-17.		5 Motor Ambulance Cars were exchanged with those of the 15th Field Ambulance.	
LA BOURSE.	12-4-17.		UNIT moved from BETHUNE to LA BOURSE.	
BAJUS.	14-4-17.		UNIT moved from LA BOURSE to BAJUS.	
"	25-4-17.		Captain H.R. DAVIES, R.A.M.C., took over Temporary Medical Charge of 13th East Yorks. Regt.	

Army Form C. 2118

WAR DIARY
INTELLIGENCE SUMMARY

(Erase heading not required.)

Instructions regarding War Diaries and Intelligence Summaries are contained in F. S. Regs., Part II. and the Staff Manual respectively. Title Pages will be prepared in manuscript.

Place	Date	Hour	Summary of Events and Information	Remarks and references to Appendices
BAJUS.	28-4-17.		BEARER DIVISION proceeded to ST. CATHERINE, ARRAS.	ex
ECOIVRES.	29-4-17.		HEADQUARTERS & TENT DIVISIONS proceeded from BAJUS to ECOIVRES.	ex
ST.CATHERINE	30-4-17.		HEADQUARTERS & TENT DIVISIONS proceeded from ECOIVRES to ST. CATHERINE, ARRAS.	ex

95TH FIELD AMBULANCE.
No. ....
Date ....

*Lieut.-Colonel, R.A.M.C.
Commanding,
95th Field Ambulance,
31st Division.*

B.E.F.

SUMMARY OF MEDICAL WAR DIARIES FOR 95th F.A., 31st Divn. 13th Corps.

1st Army.

3rd Army from 11/4/17.

WESTERN FRONT April_ May. '17.

O.C. Lt. Col. C.B. Knox.

SUMMARISED UNDER THE FOLLOWING HEADINGS.

Phase "B" Battle of Arras April_ May. 1917.

1st Period Attack on Vimy Ridge April.

2nd Period Capture of Siegfried Line May.

B.E.F.

95th F.A. 31st Divn. 13th Corps.   **WESTERN FRONT.**
O.C. Lt. Col. C.B. Knox.   **April. '17.**
1st Army.
3rd Army from 11/4/17t

Phase "B" Battle of Arras- April_ May. 1917.
1st Period Attack on Vimy Ridge April.

1917.   **Headquarters.** at Hospital Hospice - Bethune-Bethune Combine Sheet E.11.b.

April. 10th.   **Transport.** 5 Motor Ambulance Cars were exchanged with those of 15th Field Ambulance.

11th.   **Transfer.** 3rd Army.

B.E.F.

95th F.A. 31st Divn. 13th Corps.   WESTERN FRONT
O.C. Lt. Col. C.B. Knox.   April. '17.
3rd Army.

Phase "B" Battle of Arras- April- May. '17.
1st Period Attack on Vimy Ridge April.

1917.
April 11th.   Transfer. 3rd Army.
   12th.   Moves: To La Bourse.
   14th.   " To Bajus
   28th.   Moves Detachment: Br Divn. to St. Catherine-Arras.
   29th.   Moves: Headquarters and Tent Divns. to Ecoivres.
   30th.   " To St Catherine, Sheet 51.B.G.15.a.2.5.

B.E.F.

<u>95th F.A. 31st Divn. 13th Corps.</u>   <u>WESTERN FRONT.</u>
<u>O.C. Lt. Col. C.B. Knox.</u>   <u>April. '17.</u>
<u>1st Army.</u>
<u>3rd Army from 11/4/17t</u>

<u>Phase "B" Battle of Arras- April_ May. 1917.</u>
<u>1st Period Attack on Vimy Ridge April.</u>

1917.   <u>Headquarters.</u> at Hospital Hospice - Bethune-Bethune
               Combine Sheet E.11.b.

April. 10th.   <u>Transport.</u> 5 Motor Ambulance Cars were exchanged with
               those of 15th Field Ambulance.

11th.   <u>Transfer.</u> 3rd Army.

B.E.F. 2.

<u>95th F.A. 31st Divn. 13th Corps.</u>   <u>WESTERN FRONT.</u>
<u>O.C. Lt. Col. C.B. Knox.</u>   <u>April. '17.</u>
<u>3rd Army.</u>

<u>Phase "B" Battle of Arras- April- May. '17.</u>
<u>1st Period Attack on Vimy Ridge April.</u>

1917.
April 11th.   <u>Transfer.</u> 3rd Army.
    12th.   <u>Moves:</u> To La Bourse.
    14th.   " To Bajus.
    28th.   <u>Moves Detachment:</u> Br Divn. to St. Catherine-Arras.
    29th.   <u>Moves:</u> Headquarters and Tent Divns. to Ecoivres.
    30th.   " To St Catherine, Sheet 51.B.G.15.a.2.5.

Confidential

Volume XVII Vol 15

40/2230

War Diary.

95th Field Ambulance   31st Division

May 1917.

COMMITTEE FOR THE
MEDICAL HISTORY OF THE WAR
Date -7 AUG. 1917

Army Form C. 2118

WAR DIARY

INTELLIGENCE SUMMARY

MAY, 1917.

(Erase heading not required.)

Instructions regarding War Diaries and Intelligence Summaries are contained in F.S. Regs., Part II. and the Staff Manual respectively. Title Pages will be prepared in manuscript.

Place	Date	Hour	Summary of Events and Information	Remarks and references to Appendices
ST. CATHERINE.	1-5-17.		HEADQUARTERS of the UNIT at ST. CATHERINE. Sheet 51B. G.15.a.3.5.	
"	3-5-17.		D.D.M.S., XIII CORPS inspected MAIN DRESSING STATION. A party of 28 men proceeded to duty at the ADVANCED DRESSING STATION, BAILLEUL	
"	4-5-17.		1 Officer and 54 N.C.O's. and Men proceeded to the ADVANCED DRESSING STATION for duty. A party of 28 men returned from duty at the ADVANCED DRESSING STATION to the MAIN DRESSING STATION.	
"	5-5-17.		D.M.S., FIRST ARMY inspected the MAIN DRESSING STATION.	
"	7-5-17.		Major-General R. WANLESS O'GOWAN, C.B., Commanding 31st DIVISION, inspected the MAIN DRESSING STATION. Lieut. T.G. FENTON, R.A.M.C., took over temporary Medical Charge of 64 Artillery Brigade R.F.A.	
"	11-5-17.		Capt. A.E. SUTTON, M.C., R.A.M.C., took over temporary Medical Charge of 10th East Yorks.	

Army Form C. 2118

WAR DIARY
INTELLIGENCE SUMMARY
—2—
(Erase heading not required.)

Instructions regarding War Diaries and Intelligence Summaries are contained in F.S. Regs., Part II. and the Staff Manual respectively. Title Pages will be prepared in manuscript.

Place	Date	Hour	Summary of Events and Information	Remarks and references to Appendices
ST.CATHERINE.	14-5-17.		D.D.M.S., XIII CORPS inspected the MAIN DRESSING STATION. Lieut. T.G. FENTON, R.A.M.C., reported for duty from 64 Artillery Brigade, R.F.A.	WD
"	16-5-17.		1 Officer and 54 N.C.O's. and Men returned from duty at the ADVANCED DRESSING STATION.	WD
"	18-5-17.		Lieut-Colonel E.B.KNOX, R.A.M.C., proceeded on Special Leave to IRELAND. D.D.M.S., XIII CORPS inspected the MAIN DRESSING STATION.	WD
"	21-5-17.		MAIN DRESSING STATION at ST.CATHERINE (Sheet 51B. G.15.a.2.5.) handed over to 1st Field Ambulance, (R.N.D.) and proceeded by road to CAMBLIGNEUL.(Sheet 36B.W.15c. 2.5.)	WD
CAMBLIG-NEUL.	24-5-17.		Major-General R.WANLESS O'GOWAN, C.B., Commanding 31st DIVISION inspected the Camp.	WD
"	25-5-17.		Capt. R. BURGES, R.A.M.C., took over temporary Medical Charge of 13th York & Lancs. Capt. H. YOUNG, R.A.M.C. departed on Special Leave to SCOTLAND.	WD

Army Form C. 2118

WAR DIARY

INTELLIGENCE SUMMARY

(Erase heading not required.)

Instructions regarding War Diaries and Intelligence Summaries are contained in F. S. Regs., Part II. and the Staff Manual respectively. Title Pages will be prepared in manuscript.

Place	Date	Hour	Summary of Events and Information	Remarks and references to Appendices
CAMBLIGNEUL.	27-5-17.		Capt. A.E. SUTTON, M.C., R.A.M.C., reported for duty from temporary Medical Charge of 10th East Yorks.	W¾
"	29-5-17.		Capt., H.R. DAVIES, R.A.M.C., reported for duty from temporary Medical Charge of 13th East Yorks.	W¾

W.H.M.Tapken
Lieut-Colonel, R.A.M.C.,
Commanding.
95th Field Ambulance.

95th FIELD AMBULANCE
1.6.17.

B.E.F.

SUMMARY OF MEDICAL WAR DIARIES FOR 95th F.A., 31st Divn. 13th Corps.

1st Army.

3rd Army from 11/4/17.

WESTERN FRONT April- May. '17.

O.C. Lt. Col. C.B. Knox.

SUMMARISED UNDER THE FOLLOWING HEADINGS.

Phase "B" Battle of Arras April- May. 1917.

1st Period Attack on Vimy Ridge April.

2nd Period Capture of Siegfried Line May.

B.E.F.

95th F.A. 31st Divn. 13th Corps.   WESTERN FRONT.
O.C. Lt. Col. C.B. Knox.   May. '17.
3rd Army.

Phase "B" Battle of Arras- April- May. '17.
2nd Period Capture of Siegfried Line May.

1917.	
May. 3rd.	**Moves Detachment:** Party of 28 men to A.D.S.- Bailleul.
4th.	1 and 54 to A.D.S.
	Party of 28 men returned to M.D.S.
15th.	1 and 54 returned from A.D.S.
21st.	**Moves:** M.D.S. handed over to 1st F.A. (R.N.D.)- moved to Cambligneul- Sheet 36 B.W.15.c.2.5.-

B.E.F.

95th F.A. 31st Divn. 13th Corps.   WESTERN FRONT.
O.C. Lt. Col. C.B. Knox.   May. '17.
3rd Army.

Phase "B" Battle of Arras- April- May. '17.
2nd Period Capture of Siegfried Line May.

1917.
May. 3rd.   Moves Detachment: Party of 28 men to A.D.S.- Bailleul.
4th.   1 and 54 to A.D.S.
            Party of 28 men returned to M.D.S.
15th.   1 and 54 returned from A.D.S.
21st.   Moves: M.D.S. handed over to 1st F.A. (R.N.D.)- moved
            to Cambligneul- Sheet 36 B.W.15.c.2.5.-

Confidential

Volume XVIII

War Diary.

95th Field Ambulance 31st Division

June 1917.

COMMITTEE FOR THE
MEDICAL HISTORY OF THE WAR
Date 7 AUG. 1917

WAR DIARY

Army Form C. 2118

Instructions regarding War Diaries and Intelligence Summaries are contained in F.S. Regs., Part II. and the Staff Manual respectively. Title Pages will be prepared in manuscript.

(Erase heading not required.)

85TH FIELD AMBULANCE.
Date 1.7.17

Place	Date	Hour	Summary of Events and Information	Remarks and references to Appendices
CAMBLIGNEUL.	1-6-17.		HEADQUARTERS of the UNIT at CAMBLIGNEUL. Sheet 36B.W.15.c.25.	
"	5-6-17.		Captain A.E.SUTTON.M.C.RAMC. appointed Town Major of CAMBLIGNEUL.	
"	7-6-17.		Captain R.BURGES% RAMC.returned from temporary Medical Charge of 13th York and Lancaster Regiment.	
			Captain G.W.ANDERSON. RAMC. took over temporary Medical Charge of 13th. York and Lancaster Regiment.	
			Captain H.YOUNG. R.A.M.C. reported for duty from leave.	
"	9-6-17.		Captain R.BURGES.R.A.M.C. proceeded on leave for 10 days to England.	
"			Lieut.Col. E.B.KNOX.R.A.M.C. reported for duty from Special Leave to IRELAND.	
"			2.Officers and 42. N.C.Os and men proceed to take over COLLECTING POST, at GAVRELLE. Sheet 51 B. 30 a.3.3. and A.D.S.at H1.C 38.from No.2.H.N. Field Ambulance.	
"	10-6-17.		Lieut. T.G.FENTON. R.A.M.C. proceeded to take over temporary Medical Charge of 12th. York and Lancaster Regiment.	
"			Captain A.E.SUTTON. M.C. R.A.M.C. returned to duty on being relieved of his appointment as Town Major of CAMBLIGNEUL.	

Army Form C. 2118

WAR DIARY
INTELLIGENCE SUMMARY
(Erase heading not required.)

85TH FIELD AMBULANCE

Place	Date	Hour	Summary of Events and Information	Remarks and references to Appendices
ANZIN.	11-6-17.		UNIT proceeded by road to ANZIN. Mapreference 51B. G.1a.3.3. taking over accommodation from No.3.R.N.Field Ambulance.	
"	18-6-17.		This UNIT won first prize for best turn out (Ambulance and Water Cart) at 31st Divisional Horse Show.	
"	20-6-17.		Captain R.BURGES. R.A.M.C. reported for duty from leave. 1.Officer and 46.men took over A.D.S. BALLEUL ROAD.(Map Reference H.1.C.Central.)	
"	21-6-17.		This UNIT won first prize for best turn out (Ambulance and Water Cart.) at 13th Corps Horse Show.	
"	21-6-17.		Captain A.E.SUTTON.M.C. R.A.M.C. evacuated to C.C.S. (Wounded) in action	
"	24-6-17.		D.A.D.M.S. 31st Division, inspected the Headquarters of this UNIT.	
"			1st, Lieut. N.M.CANTER, UNITED STATES MEDICAL SERVICE RESERVE. reported for duty with this Unit.	
"	25-6-17.		This UNIT won first prize for best turn out, (Ambulance and Water Cart) at 1st, Army Horse Show.	
"	26th-6-17.		Lieut.T.G.FENTON.R.A.M.C. reported for duty from temporary duty with 12th, York and Lancaster Regiment.	
"	27-6-17½		1.man R.A.M.C. killed in action by enemy shell fire.	

WAR DIARY
INTELLIGENCE SUMMARY

Army Form C. 2118

(Erase heading not required.)

Place	Date	Hour	Summary of Events and Information	Remarks and references to Appendices
ANZIN.	28-6-17.		Captain. H. YOUNG. R.A.M.C. evacuated to C.C.S. (Wounded) in action.	
"			One N.C.O. and two men evacuated to C.C.S. (wounded) in action.	
	30-6-17.		A.D.M.S. 31st Division inspected Headquarters of this Unit.	

Lieut-Colonel, R.A.M.C.,
Commanding,
95th Field Ambulance,
31st Division.

95TH FIELD AMBULANCE
Date 1-7-17

Confidential

Volume XIX

War Diary.

95th Field Ambulance   31st Division

July 1917

Army Form C. 2118

95TH FIELD AMBULANCE

WAR DIARY

INTELLIGENCE SUMMARY

JULY, 1917.

(Erase heading not required.)

Instructions regarding War Diaries and Intelligence Summaries are contained in F. S. Regs., Part II. and the Staff Manual respectively. Title Pages will be prepared in manuscript.

Place	Date	Hour	Summary of Events and Information	Remarks and references to Appendices
ANZIN.	1.7.17.		HEADQUARTERS of the UNIT at ANZIN, Map reference 51B. G.1.a.3.3. ADVANCED DRESSING STATION at M.4.c.6.5. and B.26.c.6c. A.D.S. at B.25.d. Major-General R. WANLESS O'GOWAN, C.B., Commanding 31st Division and the A.D.M.S 31st Division inspected the Headquarters of the Unit.	CK
"	2.7.17.		Captain E. ROGERSON, R.A.M.C. reported for duty from No. 2 Stationary Hospital.	CK
MAROEUIL.	4.7.17.		UNIT proceeded by road to MAROEUIL, Map reference 51C.L.4.a.2.9.	CK
"	5.7.17.		D.A.D.O.S., 31st Division inspected the Headquarters of the Unit. Captain E. ROGERSON, R.A.M.C., proceeded to take over temporary Medical Charge of 14th York & Lancs. Regt.	CK
"	7.7.17.		Captain H.YOUNG, R.A.M.C. rejoined this Unit on discharge to duty from No. 30 C.C.S.	CK
"	8.7.17.		Captain H.YOUNG, R.A.M.C. proceeded to take over temporary Medical Charge of 10th East Yorks. Regt.	CK
"	12.7.17.		Captain H.YOUNG, R.A.M.C. reported for duty from temporary Medical Charge of 10th East Yorks. Regt.	CK

WAR DIARY

INTELLIGENCE SUMMARY

Army Form C. 2118

95TH FIELD AMBULANCE — 2 —

Place	Date	Hour	Summary of Events and Information	Remarks and references to Appendices
MAROEUIL.	13.7.17.		The UNIT took over MAIN DRESSING STATION AUX RIETZ "A.8.c.3.6." and ADVANCED DRESSING STATIONS at WILLERVAL B.3.d.5.3., VIMY (Reserve) T.25.a.9.4. LA CHAUDIERE S.18.c.9.3. and LOADING POST at BOIS CARRE B.7.c.4.5. (Maps 51B. N.W. and 36C. S.W.)	CK
"	20.7.17.		Captain R. BURGES, R.A.M.C. assumed temporary Medical Charge of 18th West Yorks. Captain E. ROGERSON, R.A.M.C. reported for duty from temporary Medical Charge of 14th Work & Lancs. Regt.	CK CK
"	23.7.17.		A.D.M.S., 31st Division inspected MAIN DRESSING STATION.	CK
"	25.7.17.		Captain H.R. DAVIES, R.A.M.C. proceeded for duty with FIFTH ARMY.	CK
"	31.7.17.		Major-General R. WANLESS O'GOWAN, C.B., Commanding 31st Division inspected HEADQUARTERS. D.M.S., FIRST ARMY, accompanied by D.D.M.S. XIIIth CORPS inspected HEADQUARTERS. C.R.E., 31st Division inspected the NISSEN HUTS at HEADQUARTERS. A.D.M.S., 31st Division inspected MAIN DRESSING STATION, AUX RIETZ.	CK

95TH FIELD AMBULANCE
Date: 1.8.17

R.B. Knox
Lieut-Colonel, R.A.M.C.
95th Field Ambulance
31st Division.

Confidential
24
Aug '17

Volume XX
Vol 18

140/304.

War Diary.

95th Field Ambulance   31st Division

6 August 1917.

COMMITTEE FOR THE
MEDICAL HISTORY OF THE WAR
Date -1 OCT. 1917

Army Form C.2118
95TH AMBULANCE
No. [stamp]

WAR DIARY
or
INTELLIGENCE SUMMARY
(Erase heading not required.)

August 1914.

Place	Date	Hour	Summary of Events and Information	Remarks and references to Appendices
MAROEUIL	1.8.14		Headquarters of the Unit at MAROEUIL. Map reference 51C. L.f. A.2.9. Main Dressing Station at AUX RIETZ, A.8.C.3.6, and Advanced Dressing Stations at WILLERVAL B.3.d.5.3, VIMY (RESERVE) T.25.a.9.h, LA CHAUDIERE S.18.C.9.3, and Reading Post at BOIS CARRE B.Y.C.H.5 (Map o 51B. N.W. and 36C. S.W.)	DK
-"-	-"-		LIEUT. L.M. CANTER. U.S.M.S. reported for duty from special leave to Paris	CK
-"-	-"-		LIEUT. T.G. FENTON. R.A.M.C. proceeded to take over temporary Medical Charge of 10 EAST YORKS. vice CAPT. J.N. DEACON. M.C. R.A.M.C.	CK
-"-	-"-		CAPT. J.N. DEACON. M.C. R.A.M.C. reported for duty from 10 EAST YORKS	CK
-"-	4.8.14		CAPT. R. BURGES. R.A.M.C. reported for duty from temporary Medical Charge of 18 WEST YORKS.	CK
-"-	7.8.14		A.D.M.S. 31 Division inspected the Main Dressing Station at MAROEUIL.	CK
-"-	11.8.14		CAPT. W. HUNT. M.C. R.A.M.C. proceeded on leave to Ireland.	CK
-"-	12.8.14		CAPT. F.W. MOELLER. U.S.M.S. reported for duty from No. 23 General Hospital.	CK
-"-	13.8.14		D.A.D.M.S. 31 Division inspected the Main Dressing Station at MAROEUIL.	CK

WAR DIARY
INTELLIGENCE SUMMARY

Army Form C. 2118

95TH C.E. AMBULANCE

Place	Date	Hour	Summary of Events and Information	Remarks and references to Appendices
MAROEUIL			Continued.	
-"-	15.8.17		A.D.M.S, 31 Division inspected the Main Dressing Station at MAROEUIL.	XM
-"-	16.8.17		Under instructions from D.M.S, First Army, LIEUT-COL. E.B. KNOX R.A.M.C and LIEUT-COL. R. DRAKE BROCKMAN R.A.M.C. took-over and handed over the command of 95 Field Ambulance and 150 Field Ambulance respectively.	
-"-			Under instructions from A.D.M.S, 31 Division the Advanced Dressing Station at LA CHAUDIERE was handed over to 93 Field Ambulance.	XM
-"-	18.8.17		CAPT. E. ROGERSON R.A.M.C relieved LIEUT. T.G. FENTON R.A.M.C. as temporary Medical officer of 10TH EAST YORKS.	XM
-"-	19.8.17		LIEUT-COL. R.E. DRAKE BROCKMAN proceeded to England on 10days leave of absence.	XM
-"-	22.8.17		CAPT. W. HUNT, M.C. R.A.M.C returned from leave to Ireland.	XM
-"-	24.8.17		A.D.M.S, 31 Division inspected the Main Dressing Station at MAROEUIL	XM
-"-			CAPT. F.W. MOELLER. U.S.M.S transferred for duty with 94th Field Ambulance WEF.	
-"-	25.8.17		C.E. XIII Corps visited the Main Dressing Station at MAROEUIL.	WM

Army Form C. 2118

WAR DIARY
INTELLIGENCE SUMMARY
(Erase heading not required.)

Place	Date	Hour	Summary of Events and Information	Remarks and references to Appendices
MAROEUIL			Continued	
"	28.8.14		CAPT. H. YOUNG, R.A.M.C. transferred for duty with 150th Field Ambulance.	WA
"	"		CAPT. J.E.M. WIGLEY, R.A.M.C. transferred for duty from 150th Field Ambulance.	WA
"	31.8.14		LIEUT-COL. R.E. DRAKE BROCKMAN, R.A.M.C. returned from leave to England	

Frank Freeman
Lieut-Colonel, R.A.M.O.
Commanding,
95th Field Ambulance
31st Division.

95TH FIELD AMBULANCE.
No. 1
Date 1.9.14

Confidential 97

14/2438

Volume XX4

Vol 19

War Diary.

95th Field Ambulance   31st Division

September 1917.

COMMITTEE FOR THE
MEDICAL HISTORY OF THE WAR
Date −5 NOV.1917

WAR DIARY / INTELLIGENCE SUMMARY

Army Form C. 2118

96th Field Amb. — September 1914.

Place	Date	Hour	Summary of Events and Information	Remarks and references to Appendices
MAROEUIL	1.9.14		Headquarters of the Unit at MAROEUIL. Map reference 51C. L.H. a.3.9. Main Dressing station at AUX RIETZ. A.8.c.3.6. and Advanced Dressing station at WILLERVAL B.3.d.5.3. VIMY (RESERVE) T. 35.a.9.4. and standing Post at BOIS CARRÉ B.7.c.4.5. (Maps 51B N.W. and 36C. S.W.)	NW
--	3.9.14		CAPT. R. BURGES, R.A.M.C. took over Medical and Sanitary charge of 1st Infantry Labour Company and 143 Chinese Labour Company at BEURIN. One Officer and proceeded for duty with XIII Corps Signal Coy at ORVILLE.	NW
--	6.9.14		The Unit proceeded to ANZIN (51.B.G.S.a.5.3.) and took over Field Ambulance accommodation from 1/4 K. Field Ambulance.	NW
--	7.9.14		LIEUT. T.G. FENTON took over Medical and Sanitary charge of 31st Divisional Train, A.S.C.	NW
--	9.9.14		CAPT. J.E.M. WIGLEY, R.A.M.C. took over temporary Medical charge of 13 York & Lancs Regt.	NW
--	10.9.14		CAPT. R. BURGUS R.A.M.C. relinquished Medical and Sanitary charge of 1st Infantry Labour Company and 143 Chinese Labour Company. One M.O. attached to HQ Chinese Labour Company for Medical duty.	NW
--	11.9.14 / 13.9.14		LIEUT. C.M. PENNEFATHER, R.A.M.C. reported for duty from No. 48 General Hospital. CAPT. J.E.M. WIGLEY. R.A.M.C. relinquished temporary Medical charge of 13 York & Lancs Regt. and took over temporary Medical charge of 14 York & Lancs Regt.	NW

WAR DIARY or INTELLIGENCE SUMMARY

Army Form C. 2118

95th Field Ambce

Place	Date	Hour	Summary of Events and Information	Remarks and references to Appendices
ANZIN			(Continued)	
---	13.9.17		CAPT. J.N. DEACON, M.C., R.A.M.C. took over temporary Medical Charge of 13th York and Lancs Regt.	
---	16.9.17		MAJOR GENERAL R. WANLESS-O'GOWAN C.B. Commanding 31st Division, and A.D.M.S. 31st Division inspected the Headquarters of this Unit.	
---	19.9.17		CAPT. J.N. DEACON, M.C., R.A.M.C. relinquished temporary Medical Charge of 13th York and Lancs Regt.	
---	19.9.17		LIEUT. C.M. PENNEFATHER, R.A.M.C. was transferred for duty with 5th E.C.J.	
---	20.9.17		CAPT. R. BURGES, R.A.M.C. attached 93rd Field Ambulance for temporary duty.	
---	22.9.17		CAPT. H. DUNKERLEY, R.A.M.C. reported for duty from 3rd Cavalry Division.	
---	22.9.17		LIEUT. T.G. FENTON, R.A.M.C. transferred for duty with 5th E.C.J.	
---	23.9.17		CAPT. J.N. DEACON, M.C., R.A.M.C. took over Medical and Sanitary Charge of 31st Divisional Train, A.S.C.	
---	25.9.17		A.D.M.S. 31st Division inspected the Headquarters of this Unit.	
---	28.9.17		CAPT. H. DUNKERLEY, R.A.M.C. relieved CAPT. J.E.M. WIGLEY, R.A.M.C. of Medical Charge of 14th York & Lancs. Regt.	
---	---		CAPT. R. BURGES, R.A.M.C. returned from duty with 93rd Field Ambulance.	

/95th Field Ambce/ Army Form C. 2118

No. 3.

WAR DIARY
INTELLIGENCE SUMMARY

(Erase heading not required.)

Place	Date	Hour	Summary of Events and Information	Remarks and references to Appendices
ANZIN.	29/9/17		CAPT. J.E.M. WIGLEY, R.A.M.C. proceeded on 4 days special leave to Paris.	

[signature]
Lieut Colonel R.A.M.C.
Commanding
95th Field Ambulance
31st Division.

95TH FIELD AMBULANCE
C.664
30.9.17

Confidential
Oct. 1917

Volume XII
14072578
Vol 26

COMMITTEE FOR THE
MEDICAL HISTORY OF THE WAR
Date 17 JAN. 1918

War Diary.

95th Field Ambulance 31st Division

October 1917.

SECRET

WAR DIARY
~~INTELLIGENCE SUMMARY~~

(Erase heading not required.)

Army Form C. 2118

Instructions regarding War Diaries and Intelligence Summaries are contained in F.S. Regs., Part II. and the Staff Manual respectively. Title Pages will be prepared in manuscript.

95TH FIELD AMBULANCE
No. C.950   Date 1.11.17

Place	Date	Hour	Summary of Events and Information	Remarks and references to Appendices
ANZIN	1-10-17		HEADQUARTERS of the Unit at ANZIN. Map reference 51B. G.8.a.5.2.	
"	3-10-17		A.D.M.S. 31st Division inspected HEADQUARTERS of the Unit.	
"	7-10-17		LIEUT. N.M.CANTER. U.S.M.S. reported for duty from XIII Corps. Siege Ammunition Park.	
"	8-10-17		LIEUT. N.M.CANTER. U.S.M.S. took over Temporary Medical and Sanitary Charge of 11 East Yorks. Regt.	
"	11-10-17		A.D.M.S. 31st Division inspected Headquarters of the Unit.	
"	13-10-17		CAPTAIN J.N.DEACON. M.C.,R.A.M.C. took over Temporary Medical and Sanitary Charge of 18th. Durham Light Infantry.	
"	18-10-17		CAPTAIN H.DUNKERLEY.R.A.M.C. proceeded to 93rd. Field Ambulance for Temporary Duty.	
"	24-10-17		CAPTAIN H.BURGES.R.A.M.C. proceeded to ENGLAND to report to the WAR OFFICE on the 26th inst (Authority D.G.M.S. No. B1451/10 dated 9-10-17)	
"	25-10-17		LIEUT. N.M.CANTER. U.S.M.S. reported for Duty from 11th. East Yorks.Regt.	
"	26-10-17		LIEUT. N.M.CANTER. U.S.M.S. took over Temporary Medical Charge of 18th. Durham Light Infantry in relief of CAPTAIN J.N.DEACON. M.C. R.A.M.C. Lieut & Qr.Mr. W.WILSON R.A.M.C. gazetted to the rank of Captain with effect from 12-8-17 (Authority London Gazette dated 23-10-17)	
"			CAPTAIN J.N.DEACON.M.C. R.A.M.C. evacuated Sick to XIII Corps Rest Station.	

Lieut Colonel R.A.M.C.
Commanding 95th. Field Ambulance

Confidential
Nov. 1917

Volume XXIII
Vol 26

140/2578

COMMITTEE FOR THE
MEDICAL HISTORY OF THE WAR
Date 17 JAN. 1918

War Diary.

95th Field Ambulance 31st Division

November 1917.

Army Form C. 2118

WAR DIARY

~~INTELLIGENCE SUMMARY~~

SECRET.

(Erase heading not required.)

Instructions regarding War Diaries and Intelligence Summaries are contained in F.S. Regs, Part II. and the Staff Manual respectively. Title Pages will be prepared in manuscript.

95TH FIELD AMBULANCE.

Place	Date	Hour	Summary of Events and Information	Remarks and references to Appendices
ANZIN.	1/11/17		HEADQUARTERS of the Unit at ANZIN. Map reference 51B. G.8.a.5.2.	WM
"	4/11/17		Captain H. DUNKERLEY. R.A.M.C. relieved Captain J.E.M. WIGLEY. R.A.M.C. of temporary Medical Charge of 14th Bn. York and Lanc. Regt.	WM
"	8/11/17		Lieut J. McCAUSLAND. R.A.M.C. reported for duty from No.2 Docks Camp HAVRE.	WM
"	10/11/17		Captain. J.E.M. WIGLEY. R.A.M.C. proceeded to reported to. A.D.M.S. 48th. Division for Duty.	WM
"	11/11/17		Captain J.N. DEACON. R.A.M.C. discharged to duty from XIII Corps Rest Station. Lieut B.P.BURPEE. M.O.R.C., U.S.A. reported for duty from 1/2 South Midland Field Ambulance.	WM
"	12/11/17		Captain. J.N. DRACON. M.C. R.A.M.C. exchanged duties with Captain J.E.M. WIGLEY. R.A.M.C. and reported for duty with A.D.M.S. 48th. Division. Captain E. ROGERSON. R.A.M.C. transferred permanently as Medical Officer in charge 10th. East Yorks Regt.	WM
"	14/11/17		Captain. W. HUNT. M.C. R.A.M.C. and 2 N.C.O.s proceeded to R.A.M.C. School BETHUNE for a course of Training.	WM
"	15/11/17		Captain. J.E.M. WIGLEY. R.A.M.C. transferred permanently as Medical Officer in charge of 14th. Bn. York and Lanc. Regt. Captain. H.DUNKERLEY. R.A.M.C. reported for duty on relief by Captain J.E.M. WIGLEY. R.A.M.C. from 14th. Bn. York and Lanc. Regt.	WM

Army Form C. 2118

95TH FIELD AMBULANCE

WAR DIARY
INTELLIGENCE SUMMARY

(Erase heading not required.)

Instructions regarding War Diaries and Intelligence Summaries are contained in F.S. Regs., Part II. and the Staff Manual respectively. Title Pages will be prepared in manuscript.

Place	Date	Hour	Summary of Events and Information	Remarks and references to Appendices
ANZIN	16/11/17		Lieut. B.P. BURPEE. M.O.R.C. U.S.A. posted permanent Medical Officer in charge of 13th Bn. York and Lanc. Regt.	A/M
			Captain. J.R. CRAIG. R.A.M.C. transferred from 31st. Divisional Ammunition Column. for Duty.	A/M
	18/11/17		D.A.D.M.S. 31st Division inspected Headquarters of this Unit.	A/M
	20/11/17		Captain. H.DUNKERLEY. R.A.M.C. and 30 Other Ranks proceeded and took over the Advance Dressing Station GAVRELLE GUN PITS (51B. H.4.C.5.4.) from 5th. London Field Ambulanc 47th. Division. 1. N.C.O. and 2 Other Ranks took over Advanced Post Railway Cutting (51B. B.27 a.M.8 1. N.C.O. and 2 Other Ranks took over Advanced Dressing Station CHANTICLER (51B. H.1.C.5.8.)	A/M
	21/11/17		Captain. H.R.DAVIES. R.A.M.C. reported for duty from 61st Casualty Clearing Station	A/M
	22/11/17		Captain. H.R.DAVIES. R.A.M.C. took over MAIN DRESSING STATION ST.& CATHERINE from 5th. London Field Ambulance 47th. Division.	A/M
			Lieut. N.M.CANTER. R.A.M.C. was transferred from temporary Medical Charge 18th. Durham Light Infantry to 93rd. Field Ambulance for duty and is struck off the strength of this Unit accordingly.	A/M
	24/11/17		Captain. W. HUNT. M.C. R.A.M.C. and 1.N.C.O. reported for duty from R.A.M.C. School BETHUNE on completion of course of Training.	A/M

Army Form C. 2118

WAR DIARY
INTELLIGENCE SUMMARY
(Erase heading not required.)

95th FIELD AMBULANCE

Place	Date	Hour	Summary of Events and Information	Remarks and references to Appendices
ANZIN	26/11/17		Lieut. G.D. RANSOM. M.O.R.C., U.S.A. reported for duty from 1st Western General Hospital ENGLAND.	NM
	27/11/17		Captain. and Qr.Mr. W.WILSON. R.A.M.C. proceeded on 14 days leave to ENGLAND.	NM
	28/11/17		Lieut. G.D. RANSOM. M.O.R.C., U.S.A. and 1. N.C.O. proceeded to R.A.M.C. School BETHUNE for a Course of Training.	NM
	30/11/17		Lieut. J. Mc. CAUSLAND. R.A.M.C. transferred for duty to A.D.M.S. 21st. Division in relief of Captain. C.D. BOLDSWORTH. R.A.M.C. who reported for duty with this Unit.	NM
			4 Other Ranks transferred for duty with 63rd. Field Ambulance and are struck off the strength of this Unit.	NM
			Captain. H.R. DAVIES. R.A.M.C. proceeded on 14 days leave to England.	

30/11/17

[signature]
Lieut Colonel. R.A.M.C.
Commanding 95th. Field Ambulance

Confidential 23

Volume XV

Vol 22

War Diary.

95th Field Ambulance. 31st. Division

December 1917.

Army Form C. 2118

WAR DIARY
or
INTELLIGENCE SUMMARY

(Erase heading not required.)   SECRET.

Instructions regarding War Diaries and Intelligence Summaries are contained in F.S. Regs., Part II. and the Staff Manual respectively. Title Pages will be prepared in manuscript.

Place	Date	Hour	Summary of Events and Information	Remarks and references to Appendices
ANZIN.	1/12/17		HEADQUARTERS of the Unit at ANZIN. (Map reference 51B.G.8.a.5.2.) Advanced Dressing Station, GAVRELLE GUN PITS (51B.H.4.C.5.4.) Advanced Post, Railway Cutting (51B.B.27.a.4.8.) Advanced Dressing Station CHANTECLER (51B.H.1.C.5.8.) Main Dressing Station, St. CATHERINE.	
"	3/12/17		Lieut-Colonel R. E. Drake-Brockman, R.A.M.C., proceeded on 14 days' leave to England.	
"	6/12/17		Main Dressing Station at St. CATHERINE handed over to 2/2 London Field Ambulance.	
"	7/12/17		Advanced Dressing Station, GAVRELLE GUN PITS, Railway Cutting and CHANTECLER Sidings handed over to 2/3 LONDON Field Ambulance.	
"	8/12/17		Lieut. G. D. Ransom, N.O.R.C., U.S.A., and 2 N.C.Os. returned from course of instruction at R.A.M.C. School, 33 Casualty Clearing Station.	
"	16/12/17		Lieut. G. D. Ransom, N.O.R.C., U.S.A., transferred for temporary duty to 12th King's Own Yorkshire L.I. A.D.M.S., 31st Division visited Headquarters.	
"	19/12/17		Capt. C. D. Holdsworth, R.A.M.C., transferred for duty with A.D.M.S., 21st Division. Capt. J. R. Craig, R.A.M.C., proceeded for temporary duty with 14th Yorks & Lancs. Regiment. Lieut-Colonel R.E. Drake-Brockman, R.A.M.C., assumed command of Unit on return from leave to England.	
"	23/12/17		Lieut. J. B. Ball, R.A.M.C., reported for duty on arrival from Havre.	
"	24/12/17		Capt. H. R. Davies, R.A.M.C., reported for duty on return from leave to England. Lieut. J. B. Ball, R.A.M.C., transferred for temporary duty with 11th East Lancs.	
"	27/12/17		Capt. J. R. Craig, R.A.M.C., reported for duty on relinquishing temporary duty with 11th York & Lancs.	
"	28/12/17		G.O.C., 31st Division addressed the men of the Unit.	

Lieut-Colonel, R.A.M.C.,
Commanding,
95th Field Ambulance,
31st Division.

COMMITTEE FOR THE
MEDICAL HISTORY OF THE WAR

Date -8 APR 1918

WAR DIARY
or
INTELLIGENCE SUMMARY

Army Form C. 2118

(Erase heading not required.)

95th Field Ambulance

SECRET

Place	Date	Hour	Summary of Events and Information	Remarks and references to Appendices
ANZIN.	1/8		HEADQUARTERS of the Unit at ANZIN. (Map reference 51 B.3.a.5.2.)	
"	2/8		Lieut. J.B. Ball reported for duty on relinquishing temporary medical charge of the 11th East Lancashire Regiment.	
"			Lieut. J.B. Ball proceeded to take temporary medical charge of the 211th Field Company, R.E.	
"			Capt. H. Dunkerley proceeded on 14 days' leave to England	
"	6/8		Capt. J.R. Craig proceeded on 14 days' leave to England	
"	9/8		Lieut. J.D. Ransom, M.D.R.C., U.S.A., reported for duty on relinquishing temporary medical charge of the 12th King's Own Yorkshire Light Infantry.	
"			Capt. H.R. Davies proceeded for a course of instruction at the Third Army R.A.M.C. School of Instruction.	
"	13/8		Capt. A.J. Glass reported for duty on arrival from England.	
"	14/8		Lieut. J.D. Ransom, M.O.R.C., U.S.A., was posted to duty with the 11th East Lancashire Regiment, and was struck off the strength of the Unit.	
"			Capt. F.H. Moeller, M.O.R.C., U.S.A., reported to this Unit on relinquishing medical charge of the 11th East Lancashire Regiment and proceeded for duty to report for duty with the O.C. No. 20 General Hospital.	

95TH FIELD AMBULANCE
1.8.18.

95th Field Ambulance
Page 11

Army Form C. 2118

WAR DIARY
INTELLIGENCE SUMMARY
(Erase heading not required.)

SECRET.

Place	Date	Hour	Summary of Events and Information	Remarks and references to Appendices
ANZIN	17th		Capt H. Dunkerley reported for duty on arrival from leave to England.	
"	19th		Capt. H.R. Davies and 1 N.C.O. returned from a course of instruction at the 4th Army R.A.M.C. School of Instruction.	
"	20th		Lieut J.B. Ball reported for duty on relinquishing temporary medical charge of the 211th Field Company, R.E.	
"	21st		Lieut J.B. Ball assumed temporary medical charge of the 18th West Yorkshire Regiment.	
"	23rd		Capt J.R. Braig reported for duty on arrival from leave to England.	
"	23rd		Capt A.G. Glass assumed temporary medical charge of the 12th East Yorkshire Regiment.	
"	25th		Capt J.R. Braig and two N.C.Os proceeded for a course of instruction at the Third Army R.A.M.C. School of Instruction.	
"	25th		Capt H.R. Davies was posted to duty with the O.C. 61 Bnoneth Clearing Station	
"	26th		Capt H. Dunkerley assumed temporary medical charge of the 165 Brigade, R.F.A.	
"	26th		Lieut J.B. Ball reported for duty on relinquishing temporary medical charge of the 18th West Yorkshire Regiment.	
"	30th		A.D.M.S., 31st Division, inspected the Headquarters of the Unit.	

Lieut-Colonel, R.A.M.C.
Commanding,
95th Field Ambulance,
31st Division.

COMMITTEE F
MEDICAL HISTORY
Date -8 APR. 1918

Army Form C. 2118

WAR DIARY
or
INTELLIGENCE SUMMARY

(Erase heading not required.)

95th FIELD AMBULANCE.
Date: 1.3.18.

SECRET.

Place	Date	Hour	Summary of Events and Information	Remarks and references to Appendices
ANZIN	1-2-18		Headquarters of the Unit at ANZIN. (Map reference 51B.G.6.a.5.2.)	
"	2-2-18		Capt. H. DUNKERLEY reported for duty on relinquishing temporary medical charge of the 165 Brigade, R.F.A.	
"			Capt. J.R. CRAIG reported for duty on return from a Course of Instruction at the First Army R.A.M.C. School of Instruction.	
"	4-2-18		Lieut. J.B. BALL assumed temporary medical charge of the 170 Brigade, R.F.A.	
"	6-2-18		Capt. W. HUNT, M.C., proceeded on six days" leave to Paris.	
"			Capt. H. DUNKERLEY proceeded for a course of instruction at the First Army R.A.M.C. School of Instruction.	
"	12-2-18		Capt. W. HUNT, M.C., reported for duty on return from six days" leave to Paris.	
"	15-2-18		Capt. J.E.M. WIGLEY reported for duty on transfer from the 14th Yorks & Lancs.Regt.	
"	16-2-18		Capt. W.L. SMITH, M.O.R.C., U.S.A., reported for duty on transfer from the 13th East Yorks Regiment.	
"			Capt. H. DUNKERLEY reported for duty on return from a course of instruction at the First Army R.A.M.C. School of Instruction.	
"	17-2-18		Capt. J.E.M. WIGLEY proceeded to report for duty with the A.D.M.S.,56th Division.	
"			Capt. A.G. GLASS reported for duty on relinquishing temporary medical charge of the 12th East Yorkshire Regiment.	
"	19-2-18		Capt. J.R. CRAIG assumed temporary medical charge of 13th Bn. York & Lancs.Regt.	
"			Capt. E.C. CUNNINGTON reported for duty on transfer from 12th Bn. York & Lancs.Regt.	
"	20-2-18		A.D.M.S., 31st Division, inspected the Headquarters of this Unit.	
"			Capt. W. HUNT, M.C., proceeded on 30 days" leave to United Kingdom, from 21.2.18. to 23.3.18.	
"	22-2-18		Capt. W.L. SMITH, M.O.R.C., U.S.A., proceeded for a course of instruction at the First Army R.A.M.C. School of Instruction.	
"			Lieut. J.B. BALL reported for duty on relinquishing temporary medical charge of the 170th Brigade, R.F.A.	
"	28-2-18		Capt. A.G. GLASS assumed temporary medical charge of 11th Bn. East YORKSHIRE Regt.	

Lieut-Colonel, R.A.M.C.
Commanding,
95th Field Ambulance.

COMMITTEE FOR THE
MEDICAL HISTORY OF THE WAR
Date -6 JUN 1918

SECRET.

WAR DIARY
INTELLIGENCE SUMMARY

Army Form C. 2118

95TH FIELD AMBULANCE.
Date 1.4.18

Place	Date	Hour	Summary of Events and Information	Remarks and references to Appendices
ANZIN	1.3.18		Headquarters of the Unit at ANZIN (Map reference 51B G.8.a.5.2)	
HOUDELIN	2.3.18		Unit moved to HOUDELIN (36B O.29.a.8.2)	
			Capt. E.C. CUNNINGTON assumed temporary Medical Charge of 3rd Battalion Coldstream Guards	
			Capt. J.R. CRAIG reported for duty with Unit on relinquishing temporary Medical Charge of 13 Bn. York and Lancs Regiment.	
	6.3.18		Capt. W.L. SMITH, M.O.R.C., U.S.A., reported for duty with Unit on return from a course of instruction at the First Army R.A.M.C. School of Instruction	
"			Capt. W.L. SMITH, M.O.R.C., U.S.A., was posted for duty with 93rd Field Ambulance.	
			The Unit was inspected by the D.D.M.S., First Army, accompanied by the D.D.M.S. XIII Corps and the A.D.M.S. 31st Division	
"	16.3.18		Lieut. G.D. RANSOM, M.O.R.C., U.S.A., rejoined Unit on return from Hospital	
"	17.3.18		Capt. J.B. BALL assumed temporary Medical Charge of the 15th Battalion West Yorks Regiment.	
"	19.3.18		Capt. E.C. CUNNINGTON reported for duty with Unit on relinquishing temporary Medical Charge of 3rd Battalion Coldstream Guards.	
"	22.3.18		Unit moved to BLAIREVILLE (51SX.4.d.2.9), with advanced Dressing Station at HAMELINCOURT (51B S.29.d.central).	

SECRET

Army Form C. 2118

WAR DIARY
INTELLIGENCE SUMMARY
(Erase heading not required.)

Instructions regarding War Diaries and Intelligence Summaries are contained in F. S. Regs., Part II. and the Staff Manual respectively. Title Pages will be prepared in manuscript.

95TH FIELD AMBULANCE
1.4.18

Place	Date	Hour	Summary of Events and Information	Remarks and references to Appendices
BLAIREVILLE	23.3.18		Capt. H. Dunkerley, Capt. E.C. Cunnington, and 5 N.C.O.s and 2 men were killed in action, and 2 N.C.O.s and 3 men were wounded at HAMELINCOURT	NM
---	24.3.18		The A.D.S. at HAMELINCOURT was evacuated, and an Advanced Dressing Station was opened at MOYENNEVILLE (57c A.3.d.2.3)	NM
---	25.3.18		Capt. H. Dunkerley, Capt. E.C. Cunnington, and 7 Other Ranks of this Unit killed in action on 23.3.18 were buried at BLAIREVILLE (51c X.4.d.4.9).	NM
BAILLEULMONT			Headquarters of this Unit were moved to BAILLEULMONT (51c W.B.c.3.4) The A.D.S. at MOYENNEVILLE was evacuated, and an Advanced Dressing Station was opened at AYETTE (57d F.12.a.2.2) One Other Rank was wounded in action.	NM
LA CAUCHIE	26.3.18		Capt. W. Hunt, M.C. reported for duty on return from leave to the United Kingdom Headquarters of this Unit were moved to LA CAUCHIE (51c V.18.a. central) The A.D.S at AYETTE was evacuated, and an Advanced Dressing Station was opened at ADINFER (51c X.21.d.4.4) One Other Rank was wounded in action.	NM
---	27.3.18		The A.D.S. at ADINFER was evacuated, and an Advanced Dressing Station was opened at RANSART (51c X.8.C.2.2.)	NM
---	27.3.18		Lieut. G.D. Ransom, M.O. R.C., U.S.A., assumed temporary Medical Charge of the 4th Grenadier Guards.	NM
---	29.3.18		One Other Rank was wounded in action	NM

Lieut-Colonel, R.A.M.C.
Commanding
95th Field Ambulance
31st Division.

SECRET.

WAR DIARY

INTELLIGENCE SUMMARY

Army Form C. 2118

Place	Date	Hour	Summary of Events and Information	Remarks and references to Appendices
LA CAUCHIE	31.3.18		Advanced Dressing Station at RANSART handed over to the 92 Field Ambulance, and move completed by 3 p.m., squads of this Unit being relieved at the R.A.Ps and relay posts by squads of the 92nd Field Ambulance	Nil

K. N. Rutherford
Lieut-Colonel, R.A.M.C.
Commanding,
95th Field Ambulance
81st Division.

140/2902

WAR DIARY

SECRET. INTELLIGENCE SUMMARY.
(Erase heading not required.)

Army Form C. 2118

95TH FIELD AMBULANCE 1.5.1918

Place	Date	Hour	Summary of Events and Information	Remarks and references to Appendices
LA CAUCHIE	1/4/18	—	The Unit moved from LA CAUCHIE (51c.V.18.a.Central) to WARLUZEL (51c.O.27.c.Central)	
WARLUZEL	2/4/18	—	The Unit moved from WARLUZEL to TINCQUES (36B.U.29.c.4.2)	
TINCQUES	4/4/18	—	CAPT. A.G. GLASS, R.A.M.C., reported for duty with this Unit on relinquishing temporary medical charge of 11th Bn. East Yorkshire Regiment	
"	5/4/18	—	LIEUT. G.D. RANSOM, M.O.R.C., U.S.A., reported for duty with this Unit on relinquishing temporary medical charge of 4th Bn. Grenadier Guards.	
"	6/4/18	—	LIEUT. R.B. BRITTON, R.A.M.C. and LIEUT. V. MARCUCCI, M.O.R.C., U.S.A., reported for duty with this Unit on arrival from England.	
"	7/4/18	—	The Unit moved from TINCQUES to AUBIGNY and took over the XIII. Corps Rest Station (51c.E.1.c.5.3) and the XIII. Corps Officers' Rest Station (51c.D.12.a.4.6) from the 2/3 London Field Ambulance	
AUBIGNY	7/4/18	—	CAPT. W.C.C. KIRKWOOD, R.A.M.C., reported for duty with this Unit on transfer from the 93rd Field Ambulance.	
"	8/4/18	—	The D.D.M.S. XIII. Corps, visited the Headquarters of this Unit. CAPT. A.G. GLASS, R.A.M.C., assumed temporary medical charge of the 31st Divisional Royal Engineers. The A.D.M.S., 31st Division, visited this Unit.	
"	9/4/18	—	The A.D.M.S., 31st Division, visited the XIII. Corps Rest Station	
"	10/4/18	—	A. and C. Sections of this Unit moved to TINCQUES for embussing for a northern destination. The transport proceeded by road for the same destination.	

WAR DIARY

INTELLIGENCE SUMMARY

Army Form C. 2118

Page 2

95TH FIELD AMBULANCE
Date 1.5.1918.

Place	Date	Hour	Summary of Events and Information	Remarks and references to Appendices
STRAZEELE	11/4/18		A and C. Sections of the Unit, and the transport, arrived at STRAZEELE (NORD) (Sheet 36A E.4.a.4.10)	XIII
" "	12/4/18		Rest. Sub-Divisions of A and C. Sections and the transport proceeded to HONDEGHEM (Sheet 27.V.2.d.7.6) MAJOR J. R. CRAIG, R.A.M.C. took charge of the A.D.S. at VIEUX BERQUIN (Sheet 36A N.E. E.24.a.6.5) until bearer section from the Field Ambulance A.D.S. at E.24.a.6.5. evacuated to E.16.a.0.7. One Other Rank killed in action, two Other Ranks died of wounds received in action, and One Other Rank was wounded in action at VIEUX BERQUIN	XIV
HONDEGHEM	13/4/18		Headquarters of the Unit were moved to HONDEGHEM. A.D.S. at E.16.a.0.7. evacuated to E.9.a. central	XIV
" "	14/4/18		T/CAPT. H. DUNKERLEY and CAPT. W. HUNT, M.C. (S.R.) to be Acting Majors whilst Commanding Sections of Field Ambulances, promotion dating from 4.1.18 Rest Sub-Divisions moved from HONDEGHEM to BORRE Railway Siding (Sheet 27 W.13.a.3.8.) A.D.M.S. 31st Division visited the Unit CAPT. W.C.C. KIRKWOOD, R.A.M.C. was evacuated sick to No.15 C.C.S One Other Rank killed in action and One Other Rank wounded in action A.D.S. at E.9.a. central evacuated to D.18.b.8.4.	XV
" "	16/4/18		B Section handed over the XIII Corps Rest Station to No.54 C.C.S., and the XIII Corps Officers Rest Station to No.4 C.C.S., and proceeded to join the Unit at W.13.a.3.8	XVI
" "	16/4/18		B Section arrived at W.13.a.3.8. A.D.S. at D.18.b.8.4 evacuated, and the bearer sub-division returned to W.13.a.3.8	XVII

Army Form C. 2118

WAR DIARY

INTELLIGENCE SUMMARY

Page 3

(Erase heading not required.)

Instructions regarding War Diaries and Intelligence Summaries are contained in F.S. Regs., Part II. and the Staff Manual respectively. Title Pages will be prepared in manuscript.

SECRET

95TH FIELD AMBULANCE
1. 5. 1918

Place	Date	Hour	Summary of Events and Information	Remarks and references to Appendices
HONDEGHEM	17th		Unit less transport, moved from BORRE Railway Siding to Beaver Camp (Sheet 27 V.4.c.2.5)	
"	18th		LIEUT. G.D. RANSOM, M.O.R.C., U.S.A., was detailed to take temporary medical charge of the Second Army Reinforcement Working Party.	
"	19th		Unit moved to WALLON CAPPEL (Sheet 27 U.29.c.5.2). MAJOR W. HUNT, M.C., R.A.M.C. with bearer subdivision, took over the Collecting Post at Sheet 36 A. D.30. a.4.4.	
WALLON CAPPEL	20th		A.D.M.S., 31st Division, visited the Unit.	
"	22nd		LIEUT. R.B. BRITTON, R.A.M.C., assumed temporary medical charge of the 2nd Battalion Irish Guards. A.D.M.S., 31st Division, visited the Unit.	
"	23rd		LIEUT. G.D. RANSOM, M.O.R.C., U.S.A., reported for duty on relief from temporary medical charge of the Second Army Reinforcement Working Party. LIEUT. E.F. THOMAS, R.A.M.C., reported for duty with this Unit on transfer from No.72 General Hospital. D.A.D.M.S., Second Army, and A.D.M.S., 31st Division, visited this Unit.	
"	24th		A.D.M.S., 31st Division, visited the Unit.	
"	25th		LIEUT. G.D. RANSOM, M.O.R.C., U.S.A., assumed temporary medical charge of the 4th Battalion Grenadier Guards. A.D.M.S., 31st Division, visited the Unit.	

WAR DIARY

SECRET. INTELLIGENCE SUMMARY Page 4

Army Form C. 2118

Place	Date	Hour	Summary of Events and Information	Remarks and references to Appendices
WALLON CAPPEL	26/4/18		A.D.M.S., 31st Division, visited the Unit.	XXM
" "	27/4/18		The Unit moved from Wallon Cappel to Hondeghem Beaver Camp (Sheet 27 V.4.c.2.6) on relief by the 88th Field Ambulance, and opened a Post for the reception of sick and wounded.	XXM
HONDEGHEM (Sheet 27 V.4.c.2.6)	28/4/18		A.D.M.S., 31st Division, visited the Unit.	XXM
" "	30/4/18		Headquarters of Unit at Sheet 27 V.4.c.2.6.	XXM

A.P. Scale Buchanan
Lieut-Colonel, R.A.M.C.
Commanding.
95th Field Ambulance,
31st Division.

Confidential MY

Volume XXIX
WO 27
16 of 283

War Diary.
95th Field Ambulance.

May, 1918.

COMMITTEE FOR THE
MEDICAL HISTORY OF THE WAR
9 JUL 1918

Army Form C. 2118.

WAR DIARY
or
INTELLIGENCE SUMMARY.
SECRET.

(Erase heading not required.)

Instructions regarding War Diaries and Intelligence Summaries are contained in F. S. Regs., Part II. and the Staff Manual respectively. Title pages will be prepared in manuscript.

Place	Date	Hour	Summary of Events and Information	Remarks and references to Appendices
HONDEGHEM	1/5/18		Headquarters of the Unit at HONDEGHEM (Sheet 27 V.4.c.2.6.).	
"	5/5/18		A.D.M.S., 31st. Division. held a Medical Board at the Headquarters of this Unit.	
"	9/5/18		The accommodation of this Field Ambulance was functioned as a Main Dressing Station, and the Unit became responsible for the evacuation of cases from the Advanced Dressing Station at CAESTRE (W.3.a.central).	
"	10/5/18		A.D.M.S., 31st. Division visited the Main Dressing Station.	
"	11/5/18		A.D.M.S., 31st. Division inspected the Main Dressing Station.	
"	12/5/18		A.D.M.S., 31st. Division. held a Medical Board at the Main Dressing Station.	
"	14/5/18		D.M.S. 2nd. Army accompanied by the D.D.M.S. 15th. Corps. and the A.D.M.S., 31st. Division. inspected the Main Dressing Station.	
"	15/5/18		Lieut Colonel. R.E.Drake-Brockman. R.A.M.C. proceeded on 14days leave to England. Major W.Hunt. M.C. R.A.M.C. assumed command of the Unit during the temporary absence of the Officer Commanding. Lieut F.L.Rigby. R.A.M.C. reported for duty with this Unit on transfer from the 98th. Field Ambulance.	
"	16/5/18		A.D.M.S., 31st. Division. visited the Main Dressing Station.	
"	18/5/18		A.D.M.S., 31st. Division.inspected the personnel and transport of this Unit.	
"	19/5/18		A.D.M.S., 31st. Division. held a Medical Board at the Main Dressing Station.	
"	20/5/18		Lieut. G.C.Cossar. R.A.M.C. reported for duty with this Unit on transfer from the 59th Division.	

WAR DIARY or INTELLIGENCE SUMMARY

Army Form C. 2118.

SECRET.

(Erase heading not required.)

Place	Date	Hour	Summary of Events and Information	Remarks and references to Appendices
HONDEGHEM	20/5/18		Captain. A.G.Glass. R.A.M.C. was posted to Medical Charge of the 31st. Divisional. Royal Engineers. and is struck off the strength of this Unit accordingly. Lieut. R.B.Britton. R.A.M.C. was posted to the Medical Charge of the 2nd. Bn. Irish Guards. and is struck off the strength of this Unit accordingly. Lieut G.D.Ransom. M.O.R.C.; U.S.A. was posted to the Medical Charge of the 4th. Bn. Grenadier Guards. and is struck off the strength of this Unit accordingly.	
BEAUMONT	24/5/18		This Field Ambulance was relieved by 1st South African Field Ambulance and proceeded to BEAUMONT. (A.24.b.9.9.) and took over the site from the 28th. Field Ambulance. Captain. G.Rainford. R.A.M.C. reported for duty with this Unit on transfer from the 59th Division.	
"	25/5/18		A.D.M.S. 31st. Division inspected the Headquarters of this Unit. Lieut E.F.Thomas R.A.M.C. and one N.C.O. proceeded to WO2 Army Gas School for a course of instruction.	
"	26/5/18		A.D.M.S. 31st. Division. inspected the Headquarters of this Unit.	
"	29/5/18		Lieut Colonel. R.E.Drake-Brockman. R.A.M.C. returned from 14 days Leave to England.	
"	30/5/18		Headquarters of the Unit at BEAUMONT (A.24.b.9.9.)	
			Honours and Awards:- The following Officer N.C.O.'s and Men of this Unit have been awarded the undermentioned Decorations. Military Cross, Major J.R.Craig, R.A.M.C.; Distinguished Conduct Medal, No. 68705 Acting Sergeant H.L.Dingwall, R.A.M.C.; Military Medals, No. 45907 acting Staff Sergt. A.Linton. No.68676 Private. J. Brooks, No.68631 Private J.L. Gaukroger., No. 101193 Private J.W. Hickingbotham., No. 68890 Private W.Ball. R.A.M.C.	

Lieut-Colonel, R.A.M.C.
Commanding,
95th Field Ambulance
31st Division.

95TH FIELD AMBULANCE

140/3076.

95th F.A.

June 1918.

WAR DIARY
or
INTELLIGENCE/SUMMARY

(Erase heading not required.)

Army Form C. 2118

SECRET.

Place	Date	Hour	Summary of Events and Information	Remarks and references to Appendices
BEAUMONT	1/6/18.		Headquarters of the Unit at BEAUMONT (Sheet 36 A.A.24b.9.9.) Six other ranks, R.A.M.C., reinforcements reported for duty.	
"	2/6/18.		A.D.M.S., 31st Division, visited this Unit. Lieut. G.C. GOSSAR, R.A.M.C., and one N.C.O., proceeded to the XV Corps Anti-Gas School for a course of instruction.	
"	3/6/18.		KING'S BIRTHDAY HONOURS:- The Distinguished Service Order was bestowed on Lieut-Colonel R.E. DRAKE-BROCKMAN, R.A.M.C.	
"	4/6/18.		This Field Ambulance opened for the reception of sick patients. Promotion:- Capt. (Acting Major) W. HUNT, M.C., S.R., R.A.M.C. to be Lieut. and temporary Captain from the 1.6.18. (Authority :- "London Gazette" dated 4th June, 1918.)	
"	5/6/18.		Admitted - Sick - Officers 2. Other Ranks 10. Prevailing disease, Influenza. A.D.M.S., 31st Division, visited this Unit.	
"	6/6/18.		Admitted - Sick - Other Ranks 14. Prevailing disease, V.D.G. A.D.M.S., 31st Division, visited this Unit.	
"	7/6/18.		Admitted - Sick - Other Ranks 28. Prevailing disease, Influenza. Lieut. G.C. GOSSAR, R.A.M.C., and one N.C.O. returned to duty from a course of instruction at the XV Corps Anti-Gas School.	
LANNOY CHATEAU, Nr.LUMBRES.	8/6/18.		Admitted - Sick - Officers 1; Other Ranks 53. Prevailing disease, Malaria. The Ambulance site at Beaumont was handed over to the 93rd Field Ambulance. The Transport and Personnel proceeded to LANNOY CHATEAU, near LUMBRES, and took over the Divisional Rest Station from the 93rd Field Ambulance, with one Officer (Lieut-Colonel W.D. COLES, 15th West Yorks) and 99 other ranks - patients. A Medical Inspection Room at LUMBRES was taken over from the 93rd Field Ambulance.	

Army Form C. 2118.

Sheet 2.

WAR DIARY
or
INTELLIGENCE/SUMMARY

SECRET.

(Erase heading not required.)

Instructions regarding War Diaries and Intelligence Summaries are contained in F.S. Regs., Part II. and the Staff Manual respectively. Title pages will be prepared in manuscript.

Place	Date	Hour	Summary of Events and Information	Remarks and references to Appendices
LANNOY CHATEAU, near LUMBRES.	9/6/18		Admitted – Sick – Other Ranks 70. Prevailing disease – Malaria. A.D.M.S., 31st Division, held a conference of Medical Officers at the Headquarters of this Unit. The A.A. and Q.M.G. 31st Division, inspected the Headquarters of this Unit. One N.C.O. reinforcement reported for duty.	
"	10/6/18		Admitted – Sick – Officers 1, Other Ranks 19. Prevailing disease, Malaria. A.D.M.S., 31st Division, visited the Unit and inspected Malaria patients.	
"	11/6/18		Admitted – Sick – Officers 1, Other Ranks 56. Prevailing Disease, Malaria.	
"	11/6/18		The Area Commandant of Lumbres visited the Unit.	
"	12/6/18		Admitted – Sick – Other Ranks 55. Prevailing disease, Malaria.	
"	13/6/18		Admitted – Sick – Other Ranks 94. Prevailing disease, Malaria. Five other Ranks, R.A.M.C., were exchanged with five Other Ranks, R.A.M.C., from the 93rd Field Ambulance.	
"	14/6/18		Admitted – Sick – Other Ranks 48. Prevailing disease, Malaria. One Other Rank, R.A.M.C., exchanged with one Other Rank, R.A.M.C., from 27th Field Ambulance. Five Other Ranks, R.A.M.C., reinforcements reported for duty.	
"	15/6/18		Admitted – Sick – Officers 1, Other Ranks 37. Prevailing disease, Malaria. A.D.M.S., 31st Division, inspected the Unit. Lieut. E.F. THOMAS, R.A.M.C., proceeded on 14 days' leave to the United Kingdom. Lieut. E.L. RIGBY, R.A.M.C., Lieut. G.C. COSSAR, R.A.M.C., and 21 Other Ranks proceeded for temporary duty with No. 18 C.C.S. One Other Rank, R.A.M.C., was detailed for temporary duty with No. 4 Squadron, R.A.F., Longuenesse.	
"	16/6/18		Admitted – Sick – Officers 2, Other Ranks 98. Prevailing disease, Malaria.	

Army Form C. 2118.

WAR DIARY
or
INTELLIGENCE SUMMARY.

SECRET.

(Erase heading not required.)

Instructions regarding War Diaries and Intelligence Summaries are contained in F.S. Regs., Part II. and the Staff Manual respectively. Title pages will be prepared in manuscript.

Sheet 3.

Place	Date	Hour	Summary of Events and Information	Remarks and references to Appendices
LANNOY CHATEAU, near LUMBRES.	17/6/18.		Admitted - Sick - Other Ranks 38. Prevailing Disease, Malaria. Medical Inspection Room at Lumbres closed.	
	"		KING'S BIRTHDAY HONOURS:- Meritorious Service Medals were awarded No. 59489 Sergt-Major C.G. Gwynn, R.A.M.C., and No. T 2/11301 S.S.M., J. Hutton, A.S.C.	
"	18/6/18.		Admitted - Sick - Other Ranks 5. Prevailing disease, Influenza.	
	"		The Medical and Sanitary Charge of the Refugees' Camp, Lumbres, was taken over by this Unit. Capt. G. RAINFORD, R.A.M.C., was detailed for temporary duty with 93rd Field Ambulance.	
"	19/6/18.		Admitted - Sick - Other Ranks 19. Prevailing disease Influenza.	
	"		Lieut. V. MARCUCCI, M.O., R.C., U.S.A., proceeded to take over the Medical Charge of the 2nd Battalion, Loyal North Lancashire Regt.	
"	20/6/18.		Admitted - Sick - Other Ranks 7. Prevailing disease, Influenza.	
	"		Capt. G. RAINFORD, R.A.M.C., returned to duty from 93rd Field Ambulance.	
"	21/6/18.		Admitted - Sick - Other Ranks 5. Prevailing disease, Influenza.	
"	22/6/18.		Admitted - Sick - Other Ranks 4. Prevailing disease, Influenza.	
	"		This Unit handed over the Divisional Rest Station at LANNOY CHATEAU to the 88th Field Ambulance, and took over the Divisional Rest Station at Sheet 36A.C.5.a.8.9., from the 88th Field Ambulance.	
WALLON CAPPEL.			Capt. G. RAINFORD, R.A.M.C., and eight Other Ranks took over a Sick Post at PONT ASQUIN. One N.C.O. and one Other Rank relieved personnel of the 88th Field Ambulance at the District Sick Post (Sheet 36 A.C.18 C. Central.)	
"	"		A.D.M.S., 51st Division inspected the Divisional Rest Station.	
"	23/6/18.		Admitted - Sick - Officers 2, Other Ranks 79. Prevailing disease, Influenza.	
"	"		Two N.C.O's and five Other Ranks relieved personnel of the 88th Field Ambulance at the Corps Walking Wounded Collecting Station (Sheet 27.U.19.a.5.0.)	
"	"		A.D.M.S, 51st Division, visited the Divisional Rest Station.	

Army Form C. 2118.

Sheet 4

WAR DIARY
or
INTELLIGENCE/SUMMARY.

SECRET.

(Erase heading not required.)

Instructions regarding War Diaries and Intelligence Summaries are contained in F.S. Regs., Part II. and the Staff Manual respectively. Title pages will be prepared in manuscript.

Place	Date	Hour	Summary of Events and Information	Remarks and references to Appendices
WALLON CAPPEL.	24/6/18.		Admitted – Sick – Officers 2, Other Ranks 77. Prevailing disease, Influenza.	
EBBLINGHEM.	25/6/18.		Admitted – Sick – Officers 1, Other Ranks 64. Prevailing disease, Influenza. This Unit handed over the Divisional Rest Station at Sheet 36 A.C.5.a.8.9., to the 93rd Field Ambulance, for a Main Dressing Station, and opened a Divisional Rest Station at EBBLINGHEM, (Sheet 27 T.18.a.9.9.) One N.C.O. and one Other Rank were relieved by personnel of the 93rd Field Ambulance at the District Sick Post (Sheet 36 A.C.18.c.central.)	
"	26/6/18.		Admitted – Sick – Officers 2, Other Ranks 75. Prevailing disease, Influenza. A.D.M.S., 31st Division, inspected the Divisional Rest Station. Capt. G. RAINFORD, R.A.M.C., was transferred for duty with the A.D.M.S., 30th Division. Two N.C.O's and five Other Ranks were relieved by personnel of the 93rd Field Ambulance at the Corps Walking Wounded Collecting Station (Sheet 27 U.19.a.5.0.)	
"	27/6/18.		Admitted – Sick – Other Ranks 57. Prevailing disease, Influenza. C.R.E., XV Corps Troops 2nd Army, visited the Divisional Rest Station. HONOURS:- The Field Marshal Commanding-in-Chief the British Armies in France, under the authority of His Majesty the King, awarded the Military Cross to Lieut. G.C. COSSAR, R.A.M.C. Two Bearer Sections reported to the 93rd Field Ambulance for temporary duty in the "Borderland" operations.	
"	28/6/18.		Admitted – Sick – Other Ranks 35. Prevailing disease, Influenza.	
"	29/6/18.		Admitted – Sick – Other Ranks 30. Prevailing disease, Influenza.	

Sheet 5.

Army Form C. 2118.

SECRET.

WAR DIARY
or
INTELLIGENCE/SUMMARY.
(Erase heading not required.)

Instructions regarding War Diaries and Intelligence Summaries are contained in F. S. Regs., Part II. and the Staff Manual respectively. Title pages will be prepared in manuscript.

Place	Date	Hour	Summary of Events and Information	Remarks and references to Appendices
EBBLINGHEM.	30/6/18.		Admitted - Sick - Other Ranks 46. Prevailing disease, Influenza.	
"	"		Total Admissions - Sick - ... ... 1365. Evacuations. ... ... 930. Discharged to duty. ... ... 201.	
"	"		Two Bearer Sections returned to Headquarters on completion of their duty in the "Borderland" operations.	
"	"		Headquarters of Unit at Sheet 27 T.18.a.9.9.	

Lieut.-Colonel, R.A.M.C.
COMMANDING
95TH FIELD AMBULANCE.

95TH FIELD AMBULANCE.
No. F/191
Date 1.7.18

140/3131

COMMITTEE FOR THE
MEDICAL HISTORY OF THE WAR
Date

WAR DIARY
or
INTELLIGENCE/SUMMARY/

Army Form C. 2118

SECRET 95 - 2nd Aust

(Erase heading not required.)

Place	Date	Hour	Summary of Events and Information	Remarks and references to Appendices
EBBLINGHEM	1.7.18.		Headquarters of Unit at Divisional Rest Station (Sheet 27 T.18.a.9.o). Admitted - Sick - Officers 1, Other Ranks 30. Prevailing Disease, Influenza.	
"	2.7.18.		Admitted - Sick - Officers 1, Other Ranks 31. Prevailing Disease, Influenza. A.D.M.S., 31st Division, visited the Unit. Lieut. E.F. THOMAS, R.A.M.C., reported for duty on return from leave to the United Kingdom.	
"	3.7.18.		Admitted - Sick - Officers 1, Other Ranks 29. Prevailing Disease, Influenza.	
"	4.7.18.		Admitted - Sick - Other Ranks 12. Prevailing Disease, Influenza. Lieut. G.C. COSSAR, M.C., R.A.M.C., reported for duty on return from temporary duty with No. 18 Casualty Clearing Station. Three American Officers and five other ranks American Troops reported for instruction at the Divisional Rest Station.	
"	5.7.18.		Admitted - Sick - Other Ranks 25. Prevailing Disease, I.C.T. Three American Officers and five Other Ranks, American Troops, were transferred to the 93rd Field Ambulance, and two American Officers and five Other Ranks, American Troops, reported for instruction at the Divisional Rest Station.	
"	6.7.18.		Admitted - Sick - Other Ranks 19. Prevailing Disease, Myalgia. D.D.M.S., XV Corps, inspected the Divisional Rest Station. Two American Officers and five Other Ranks, American Troops, were transferred to 93rd Field Ambulance, and three American Officers and four Other Ranks, American Troops, reported for instruction at the Divisional Rest Station.	
"	7.7.18.		Admitted - Sick - Officers 1, Other Ranks 19. Prevailing Disease, Influenza.	
"	8.7.18.		Admitted - Sick - Other Ranks 13. Prevailing Disease, I.C.T. LIEUT. G.C. COSSAR, M.C., R.A.M.C., assumed temporary Medical Charge of the 24th Battalion Royal Welsh Fusiliers.	

Army Form C. 2118

WAR DIARY
or
INTELLIGENCE/SUMMARY//
(Erase heading not required.)

SECRET.

Instructions regarding War Diaries and Intelligence Summaries are contained in F.S. Regs., Part II. and the Staff Manual respectively. Title Pages will be prepared in manuscript.

Place	Date	Hour	Summary of Events and Information	Remarks and references to Appendices
EBBLINGHEM	9.7.18.		Admitted – Sick – Other Ranks 26. Prevailing Disease, I.C.T. Three American Officers and four Other Ranks, American Troops, were returned to their Unit on completion of instruction at the Divisional Rest Station.	
"	10.7.18.		Admitted – Sick – Other Ranks 36. Prevailing Disease, I.C.T. and Scabies.	
"	11.7.18.		Admitted – Sick – Officers 2, Other Ranks 23. Prevailing Disease, Influenza.	
"	12.7.18.		Admitted – Sick – Other Ranks 19. Prevailing Disease, I.C.T. and Scabies.	
"	13.7.18.		Admitted – Sick – Other Ranks 21. Prevailing Disease, Gastritis and I.C.T. A Lecture on Skin Disease was given at the Divisional Rest Station by Major Mc.CORMACK, R.A.M.C. The attendance included the D.D.M.S., XV Corps and A.D.M.S., 31st Division. A Working Party of 25 men of this Unit reported for duty with O.C., No. 1 Advanced Dressing Station. (Sheet 36A D.18.a.4.2.)	
"	14.7.18.		Admitted – Sick – Other Ranks 11. Prevailing Disease, Influenza.	
"	15.7.18.		Admitted – Sick – Other Ranks 17. Prevailing Disease, Influenza and Scabies.	
"	16.7.18.		Admitted – Sick – Other Ranks 27. Prevailing Disease, I.C.T.	
"	17.7.18.		Admitted – Sick – Other Ranks 24. Prevailing Disease, Influenza. LIEUT. F.L. RIGBY, R.A.M.C., and 21 Other Ranks of this Unit returned to Headquarters from temporary duty with No. 18 Casualty Clearing Station. LIEUT. F.L. RIGBY, R.A.M.C., proceeded to temporary duty with 94th Field Ambulance.	
"	18.7.18.		Admitted – Sick – Other Ranks 21. Prevailing Disease, Scabies.	
"	19.7.18.		Admitted – Sick – Other Ranks 53. Prevailing Disease, Scabies.	

Army Form C. 2118

WAR DIARY
or
INTELLIGENCE/~~SUMMARY~~ SECRET.

(Erase heading not required.)

Instructions regarding War Diaries and Intelligence Summaries are contained in F. S. Regs., Part II. and the Staff Manual respectively. Title Pages will be prepared in manuscript.

Place	Date	Hour	Summary of Events and Information	Remarks and references to Appendices
EBBLINGHEM.	20.7.18.		Admitted – Sick – Other Ranks 34. Prevailing Disease, Scabies.	
"	21.7.18.		Admitted – Sick – Other Ranks 32. Prevailing Disease, Scabies. Working Party of 25 Other Ranks of this Unit relieved by a similar party of this Unit at No. 1 Advanced Dressing Station (Sheet 36A D.18.a.4.2.)	
"	22.7.18.		Admitted – Sick – Officers 1, Other Ranks 11. Prevailing Disease, Influenza. A.D.M.S., 31st Division, inspected the Divisional Rest Station.	
"	23.7.18.		Admitted – WOUNDED – Officers 1; Sick, Other Ranks 19. Prevailing Disease, Influenza. LIEUT. F.L. RIGBY, R.A.M.C., reported for duty with this Unit on return from temporary duty with 94th Field Ambulance.	
"	24.7.18.		Admitted – Sick – Other Ranks 17. Prevailing Disease, Scabies. LIEUT. F.L. RIGBY, R.A.M.C., assumed temporary Medical Charge of the 12th Battalion Royal Scots Fusiliers.	
"	25.7.18.		Admitted – Sick – Other Ranks 22. PREVAILING DISEASE, Scabies.	
"	26.7.18.		Admitted – Sick – Other Ranks 13. Prevailing Disease, I.C.T.	
"	27.7.18.		Admitted – WOUNDED – Officers 1; Sick – Officers 2, Other Ranks 19. Prevailing Disease, Influenza. A.D.M.S., 31st Division, visited the Divisional Rest Station on the occasion of a Concert given by the "Magpies" Concert Party of the 95th Field Ambulance.	
"	28.7.18.		Admitted – Sick – Officers 1, Other Ranks 18. Prevailing Disease, Diarhoea.	
"	29.7.18.		Admitted – Sick – Other Ranks 15. Prevailing Disease, Diarhoea. Working Party of 25 Other Ranks of this Unit relieved by a similar party of this Unit at No. 1 Advanced Dressing Station (Sheet 36A D.18.a.4.2.)	

Army Form C. 2118

WAR DIARY
or
INTELLIGENCE/SUMMARY/ SECRET.
(Erase heading not required.)

Instructions regarding War Diaries and Intelligence Summaries are contained in F. S. Regs., Part II. and the Staff Manual respectively. Title Pages will be prepared in manuscript.

Place	Date	Hour	Summary of Events and Information	Remarks and references to Appendices
EBBLINGHEM.	30.7.18.		Admitted – Sick – Other Ranks, 16. Prevailing Disease, I.C.T.	
"	31.7.18.		Admitted – Sick – Officers 1, Other Ranks 25. Prevailing Disease, I.C.T. Lieut–Colonel R.E. Drake-Brockman, D.S.O., R.A.M.C., proceeded on 14 days' Special Leave to United Kingdom, and Major W. HUNT, M.C., R.A.M.C., assumed command of this Unit. No. 68887, Pte. E.G. Bonser, R.A.M.C., proceeded to report for duty with 10th East Yorks to undergo one month's attachment to an Infantry Battalion. No. 68848, Pte. W. Verrall, R.A.M.C., proceeded to report for duty with 24th Battalion Royal Welsh Fusiliers to undergo one month's attachment duty. The Corps Commander XI Army Corps has awarded the Military Medal to the under-mentioned N.C.O's of this Unit:– No. 69063 Pte. (A/Sgt.) J.H. Jones, R.A.M.C. " 24664 Cpl. A.V. Henderson, R.A.M.C. A.D.M.S., 31st. Division, visited the Unit. TOTAL ADMISSIONS – Officers, sick, 10; wounded, 2; Other Ranks, sick, 682; wounded, 1 – 695. EVACUATIONS – Officers, sick, 10; wounded, 2; Other Ranks, sick, 473; wounded, 1 – 486. DISCHARGED TO DUTY – Other Ranks, sick – 277. HEADQUARTERS of UNIT at DIVISIONAL REST STATION (map reference Sheet 27. T. 18. a.9.0.)	

95TH FIELD AMBULANCE.
No. F/332
Date 1..8..18.

(signature)
LIEUT.-COLONEL, R.A.M.C.
COMMANDING
95TH FIELD AMBULANCE.

140/3259

95 L. F. Amb.

Aug. 1918.

Army Form C. 2118

95 7n army
Vol 30

WAR DIARY
or
INTELLIGENCE/SUMMARY

(Erase heading not required.)

SECRET.

Instructions regarding War Diaries and Intelligence Summaries are contained in F. S. Regs., Part II. and the Staff Manual respectively. Title Pages will be prepared in manuscript.

Place	Date	Hour	Summary of Events and Information	Remarks and references to Appendices
EBBLINGHEM.	1.8.18.		HEADQUARTERS of UNIT at Divisional Rest Station (Sheet 27. T. 18. a. 9.0.) Admitted – Sick – Other Ranks. 21. Prevailing Disease, Scabies.	60w
"	2.8.18.		Admitted – Sick – Other Ranks. 31. Prevailing Disease, Scabies.	103+
"	3.8.18.		Admitted – Sick – Other Ranks. 20. Prevailing Disease, Scabies.	103+
"	4.8.18.		Admitted – Sick – Officers. 1. (Major. H.L. REED. 94th. Brigade Headquarters) Other Ranks. 21. Prevailing Disease, Influenza.	15r
"	5.8.18.		Admitted – Sick – Other Ranks. 27. Prevailing Disease, Scabies.	103+
"	6.8.18.		Admitted – Sick – Other Ranks. 33. Officers. 1. Prevailing Disease, Scabies. Working Party of 25 Other Ranks of this Unit relieved by a similar party of this Unit at No. 1. Advanced Dressing Station (Sheet 36. A. D. 18.a.4.2.)	W3+
"	7.8.18.		Admitted – Sick – Other Ranks. 35 Prevailing Disease, Diarrhoea.	W3+
"	8.8.18.		Admitted – Sick – Officers. – 1. Other Ranks. 29. Prevailing Disease, Debility.	W5+
"	9.8.18.		Admitted – Sick – Other Ranks. 21. Prevailing Disease, Debility.	15r
"	10.8.18.		Admitted – Sick – Other Ranks. 18. Prevailing Disease, Debility.	W3+
"	11.8.18.		Admitted – Sick – Other Ranks. 21. Prevailing Disease, Scabies. CAPTAIN. J.M. MOYES., R.A.M.C., Medical Officer in charge of the 12th. Bn. Royal Scots. Fusiliers, reported for temporary duty with this Unit.	103+
"	12.8.18.		Admitted – Sick– Other Ranks. 18. Prevailing Disease, Scabies. D.D.M.S., XV. Corps., A.D.M.S., 31st. Division, and the A.A. and Q.M.G., 31st. Division, inspected the Divisional Rest Station.	10+

1875 Wt. W593/826 1,000,000 4/15 J.B.C. & A. A.D.S.S./Forms/C. 2118.

Army Form C. 2118

WAR DIARY

INTELLIGENCE/SUMMARY

(Erase heading not required.)

Instructions regarding War Diaries and Intelligence Summaries are contained in F.S. Regs., Part II. and the Staff Manual respectively. Title Pages will be prepared in manuscript.

(2).

Place	Date	Hour	Summary of Events and Information	Remarks and references to Appendices
EBBLINGHEM.	13.8.18.		Admitted – Sick – Other Ranks. 28. Prevailing Disease, Scabies. LIEUT. E.F. THOMAS, R.A.M.C., relieved LIEUT. G.C. COSSAR, M.C., R.A.M.C., in temporary Medical Charge of the 24th Bn. Royal Welsh Fusiliers. The G.O.C. 31st. Division and A.D.M.S., 31st. Division inspected the Divisional Rest Station.	WD
"	14.8.18.		Admitted – Sick – Other Ranks. 29. Prevailing Disease, Scabies. LIEUT. G.C. COSSAR. M.C., R.A.M.C. proceeded on 14 days leave to the United Kingdom.	WD
"	15.8.18		Admitted – Sick – Other Ranks. 30. Prevailing Disease, Scabies.	WD
"	16.8.18		Admitted – Sick – Other Ranks. 27. Prevailing Disease, Scabies. Lieut Colonel R.E. DRAKE-BROCKMAN., D.S.O., R.A.M.C. returned from Special Leave to the United Kingdom. A.D.M.S., 31st. Division. visited the Divisional Rest Station. One N.C.O., R.A.M.C. reinforcement reported for duty.	
"	17.8.18.		Admitted – Sick – Other Ranks. 40. Prevailing Disease, Scabies and Diarrhoea. CAPTAIN. E.F. THOMAS., R.A.M.C. proceeded to England to report to the War Office.	
"	18.8.18.		Admitted – Sick – Other Ranks. 13. Prevailing Disease, Scabies. One N.C.O., R.A.M.C. reinforcement reported for duty. A.D.M.S., 31st. Division. visited the Divisional Rest Station.	
"	19.8.18.		Admitted – Sick – Other Ranks –33. Prevailing Disease. Debility.	
"	20.8.18		Admitted – Sick – Other Ranks. 19. Prevailing Disease, Scabies. CAPTAIN and QR. MR. W.WILSON., R.A.M.C. proceeded on 14 days leave to the United Kingdom. The G.O.C. XV. Corps. visited the Divisional Rest Station.	
"	21.8.18.		Admitted – Sick – Other Ranks. 7. Prevailing Disease, I.C.T. CAPTAIN. R. MC.KINNON. R.A.M.C. reported for duty with this Unit.	

1875 Wt. W593/826 1,000,000 4/15 J.B.C. & A. A.D.S.S./Forms/C. 2118.

Army. Form. C. 2118

WAR DIARY
INTELLIGENCE/SUMMARY/
(Erase heading not required.)

Instructions regarding War Diaries and Intelligence Summaries are contained in F. S. Regs., Part II. and the Staff Manual respectively. Title Pages will be prepared in manuscript.

Place	Date	Hour	Summary of Events and Information	Remarks and references to Appendices
EBBLINGHEM	22.8.18		Admitted - Sick - Other Ranks, 17. Prevailing Disease, Scabies. Five Other Ranks of this Unit proceeded to the XV. Corps Scabies School for a course of instruction. A Working Party of 25 Other Ranks of this Unit returned to Headquarters from Temporay Duty at No. 1. Advanced Dressing Station (Sheet 36A. D. 18. a. 4.2.)	
"	23.8.18.		Admitted - Sick - Other Ranks, 35. Prevailing Disease, Scabies.	
CAESTRE	24.8.18		This UNIT handed over the Divisional Rest Station to the 93rd. Field Ambulance, and relieved the 27th. Field Ambulance at CAESTRE, establishing HEADQUARTERS at Sheet 27.S.E. Q. 31.b.3.3., ADVANCED DRESSING STATION at Q. 32.d.3.9., DIVISIONAL COLLECTING POST at W. 6.d.95.95 and AID POST at the EMBANKMENT X. 7.a.1.2., clearing the REGIMENTAL AID POSTS at X.3. d.6.7., X. 9.c.7.3., X. 1.d.5.2., X. 5.a.5.3., X. 20.b.2.9. and X. 14.d. 9.8., A.D.M.S., 31st. Division, visited the Advanced Dressing Station.	
"	25.8.18.		Five Other Ranks returned from course of instruction at XV Corps Scabies School.	
"	26.8.18.		CAPTAIN. H.W. TAYLOR, R.A.M.C., attached 10th. Bn. EAST YORKS. REGT. reported to this Unit for Duty. This Unit won First Prize at the 31st. Divisional Horse Show for the R.A.M.C. Turnout.	
"	27.8.18.		A.D.M.S., 31st. Division, visited the Advanced Dressing Station.	
"	28.8.18.		CAPTAIN R. MACKINNON. S.R. R.A.M.C., was posted to the 93rd. Field Ambulance. and was struck off the strength of this Unit from this date. LIEUT F.L.RIGBY, R.A.M.C., was posted in Medical Charge of the 12th. Bn. Royal Scots. Fus. and was struck off the strength of this Unit from this date. CAPTAIN. J.M. MOYES, R.A.M.C., was posted to this Unit for duty, and was taken on the strength from this date. One Other Rank wounded in Action.	

Army Form C. 2118

WAR DIARY
INTELLIGENCE/SUMMARY
(Erase heading not required.)

Place	Date	Hour	Summary of Events and Information	Remarks and references to Appendices
CAESTRE.	29.8.18.		LIEUT G.C.COSSAR, M.C., R.A.M.C., reported for temporary duty with 24th. Royal Welsh Fus. on return from leave to the United Kingdom. The A.D.M.S., 31st. Division, visited the Advanced Dressing Station.	
"	30.8.18.		A.D.M.S., 31st. Division, inspected the Advanced Dressing Station.	
"	31.8.18.		HEADQUARTERS of the UNIT were moved to FLETRE (W. 6.d.95.95.), and the ADVANCED DRESSING STATION was established at METEREN (X. 9.c.7.2.) Number of Patients Admitted - Officers - Sick - 3., Other ranks - 576, Other ranks Wounded - 1. Number of Patients evacuated to C.C.S., Officers - Sick - 3., Other ranks - 320, Other Ranks Wounded - 1. Number of Other ranks discharged to duty - 179. Number of Other ranks transferred to XV. Corps Skin Centre. - 77. Number of Other ranks transferred to A.A.Dysentery Centre - 5. Number of Patients Other ranks transferred to 93rd. Field Ambulance - 60. Number of Patients remaining in Field Ambulance - Nil.	

[Stamp: 95TH FIELD AMBULANCE. 1.9.18.]

Lieut Colonel. R.A.M.C.
Commanding 95th. Field Ambulance

95th Fd. Amb.

14/3327

Army Form C. 2118

WAR DIARY
or
INTELLIGENCE/SUMMARY/

(Erase heading not required.)

SECRET.

95 Fd Amb

Vol 31

Place	Date	Hour	Summary of Events and Information	Remarks and references to Appendices
FLETRE.	1.9.18		HEADQUARTERS of Unit at FLETRE. (Sheet 27. S.E. W.6.d.95.95.)	
"	3.9.18		A.D.M.S., 31st. Division, visited HEADQUARTERS. An ADVANCED DRESSING STATION was established at S.30.c.4.8. (Sheet 28. S.W.) One Other Rank wounded.	
"	4.9.18		A.D.M.S., 31st. Division, visited HEADQUARTERS. CAPTAIN and QUARTERMASTER. W. WILSON., R.A.M.C., reported for duty on return from Leave to the United Kingdom.	
BAILLUEL	5.9.18		HEADQUARTERS of Unit were moved to BAILLUEL (Sheet 28 S.W. S.28.c.1.2.) Three Other ranks wounded.	
"	6.9.18		HEADQUARTERS of Unit were moved to Sheet 27.S.E. X.17.d.4.4.	
"	8.9.18		One Other Rank wounded.	
	9.9.18		LIEUT G.C. COSSAR, M.C., R.A.M.C., was posted to Medical Charge of 24th. Battalion Royal Welsh Fusiliers and was struck off the strength of this Unit from this date.	
"	10.9.18		One Other Rank wounded.	
FLETRE.	12.9.18		HEADQUARTERS of Unit moved to FLETRE (Sheet 27.S.E. W.6.d.95.95.) Two Other Ranks reinforcements reported for duty with this Unit.	
"	14.9.18		One Other Rank wounded.	
"	17.9.18		MAJOR. J.R. CRAIG., M.C., R.A.M.C., proceeded on 14 days leave to the United Kingdom.	

Army Form C. 2118

WAR DIARY
or
INTELLIGENCE/SUMMARY/
(Erase heading not required.)

(2)

Instructions regarding War Diaries and Intelligence Summaries are contained in F. S. Regs., Part II. and the Staff Manual respectively. Title Pages will be prepared in manuscript.

Place	Date	Hour	Summary of Events and Information	Remarks and references to Appendices
FLETRE.	18.9.18		CAPTAIN. H.W. TAYLOR, R.A.M.C., proceeded on 14 days leave to the United Kingdom.	
"	22.9.18		D.D.M.S., XV. Corps, visited the ADVANCED DRESSING STATION. LIEUT. E.J.S. BONNETT, S.R., R.A.M.C., reported for duty with this Unit on arrival from R.A.M.C., Base, ETAPLES.	
"	23.9.18		One M.T. reinforcement reported for duty with this Unit.	
"	24.9.18		One M.T. reinforcement reported for duty with this Unit. No. 68887 Pte. E.G. BONSER and No. 68848 Pte. W. VERRALL rejoined this Unit on completion of a months attachment duty with the 10th East Yorks Regiment (Candidates for Commissions)	
"	25.9.18		HEADQUARTERS of Unit moved to FAUNA FARM (Sheet 27. S.E. X.1.b.3.1.) One Other Rank wounded.	
"	27.9.18		A.D.M.S., 31st Division, visited Headquarters of Unit.	
"	28.9.18		A.D.M.S., 31st Division, visited the ADVANCED DRESSING STATION. Major W. HUNT, M.C., wounded in action, and remained at duty.	
"	30.9.18		Headquarters of Unit at FAUNA FARM (Sheet 27 S.E. X.1.b.3.1.)	

95TH FIELD AMBULANCE
No.
Date 1.10.18.

Lieut-Colonel, R.A.M.C.,
Commanding 95th Field Ambulance.

Army Form C. 2118

WAR DIARY
or
INTELLIGENCE/SUMMARY

(Erase heading not required.)

S E C R E T.

Instructions regarding War Diaries and Intelligence Summaries are contained in F.S. Regs., Part II. and the Staff Manual respectively. Title Pages will be prepared in manuscript.

Place	Date	Hour	Summary of Events and Information	Remarks and references to Appendices
FLETRE.	1.10.18.		HEADQUARTERS OF UNIT AT FAUNA FARM (Sheet 27 S.E.X.1.b.3.1.) A.D.M.S., 31st Division visited the headquarters of this Unit. D.D.M.S., XV Corps and A.D.M.S., 31st Division, visited the Advanced Dressing Station. LIEUT. T.A. KYNER, M.C., U.S.A., reported for duty with this Unit on arrival from the R.A.M.C. School, Etaples.	
"	3.10.18.		MAJOR J.R. CRAIG, M.C., R.A.M.C., reported for duty on return from leave to the United Kingdom. A.D.M.S., 31st Division, visited the headquarters of this Unit.	
"	4.10.18.		CAPT., H.W. TAYLOR, R.A.M.C., reported for duty on return from leave to the United Kingdom. LIEUT. A.W. THOMSON, M.C., U.S.A., reported for duty with this Unit on arrival from the R.A.M.C. School, Etaples. CAPT. H.W. TAYLOR, R.A.M.C., was posted for duty as M.O. i/c 10th EAST YORKS Regt., and was struck off the strength of this Unit this date.	
"	5.10.18.		LIEUT. N.B. PEACOCK, R.A.M.C., reported for duty with this Unit on arrival from the R.A.M.C. School, Etaples.	
"	6.10.18.		A.D.M.S., 31st Division, visited the headquarters of this Unit.	
"	7.10.18.		A.D.M.S., 31st Division, visited the Advanced Dressing Station.	
"	8.10.18.		LIEUT. E.J.S. BONNETT, R.A.M.C., was detailed for temporary duty with A.D.M.S., 31st Division.	
"	11.10.18.		One other rank was wounded in action.	
"	12.10.18.		MAJOR W. HUNT, M.C., R.A.M.C., proceeded on 14 days' leave to the United Kingdom. A.D.M.S., 31st Division, visited the Advanced Dressing Station.	

Army Form C. 2118.

95TH FIELD AMBULANCE
No.
Date 1.11.18

Sheet 2.

WAR DIARY
or
INTELLIGENCE/SUMMARY.
(Erase heading not required.)

SECRET.

Instructions regarding War Diaries and Intelligence Summaries are contained in F. S. Regs., Part II. and the Staff Manual respectively. Title pages will be prepared in manuscript.

Place	Date	Hour	Summary of Events and Information	Remarks and references to Appendices
FLETRE.	13.10.18.		CAPT. J.M. MOYES, R.A.M.C., was transferred for duty with the 94th Field Ambulance, and was struck off the strength of this Unit from this date.	
"	14.10.18.		One N.C.O. and two other ranks were wounded in action.	
"	16.10.18.		Headquarters of this Unit were moved from FAUNA FARM to CARLISLE LINES (Sheet 36.B.2.b.8.8.)	
CARLISLE LINES.	17.10.18.		One N.C.O. reinforcement reported for duty.	
QUESNOY.	18.10.18.		Headquarters of this Unit moved from CARLISLE LINES to QUESNOY (Sheet 36.D.10.b.8.0.) Advanced Dressing Station was moved to CROIS BLANCHE (Sheet 36.F.7.a.)	
LANNOY.	19.10.18.		Headquarters of this Unit and the Advanced Dressing Station were moved to LANNOY (Sheet 36.G.15.b.13.) and the Transport moved to BOIS BLANC (Sheet B 6.E.6.d.)	
"	20.10.18.		The Advanced Dressing Station was moved to LEERS NORD (Sheet 37.H.2.b.2.7.) A.D.M.S., 31st Division visited the Headquarters of this Unit.	
"	22.10.18.		Two other ranks reinforcements reported for duty with this Unit.	
"	24.10.18.		The Transport of this Unit proceeded from BOIS BLANC to LEERS (Sheet 37.C.12.c.2.6.)	
"	26.10.18.		The Advanced Dressing Station was handed over to the 136th Field Ambulance.	
STACEGHEM.	27.10.18.		The Unit moved from LANNOY to STACEGHEM (Sheet 29.H.30.a.2.0.) LIEUT. A.W. THOMSON, M.C., U.S.A., proceeded to 93rd Field Ambulance for temporary duty.	
"	28.10.18.		A.D.M.S., 31st Division, visited the Headquarters of this Unit.	

Army Form C. 2118

WAR DIARY
or
INTELLIGENCE SUMMARY

SECRET

(Erase heading not required.)

Place	Date	Hour	Summary of Events and Information	Remarks and references to Appendices
STACEGHEM.	29.10.18.		MAJOR J.M. MOYES, R.A.M.C., and 29 Other Ranks were detailed for duty at the Civilian Hospital Du FORTE, COURTRAI.	
"	30.10.18.		LIEUT. A.W. THOMSON, M.C., U.S.A., and LIEUT. T.A. KYNER, M.C., U.S.A., were detailed to report for duty with the A.D.M.S., 9th Division at HARLEBEKE. A Bearer Party of 3 N.C.O's and 40 men were detailed for duty with the 93rd Field Ambulance.	
"	31.10.18.		MAJOR J.R. CRAIG, M.C., R.A.M.C., was detailed to take temporary charge of detraining post (Sheet 28.L.13) during operations.	
"	"		MAJOR J.M. MOYES, R.A.M.C., returned to the 94th Field Ambulance on completion of temporary duty with this Unit.	
"	"		A Divisional Rest Station for 50 cases was opened by this Unit at STACEGHEM.	
"	"		HEADQUARTERS of Unit at Sheet 29.H.30.a.2.0.	
	31.10.18.		HONOURS:- The Corps Commander XVth Corps awarded the MILITARY MEDAL to the under-mentioned N.C.O's of this Unit:- No. 34858 Sgt. (A/s/Sgt.)H.J.D. PORTER, R.A.M.C. " M2/021596 Cpl. J. JOHNSON, M.T., A.S.C.	

Lieut-Colonel, R.A.M.C.,
Commanding 95th Field Ambulance.

No. 95-7. a.

COMMITTEE FOR THE
MEDICAL HISTORY OF THE WAR
6 MAR. 1919
Date

Army Form C. 2118

WAR DIARY
or
INTELLIGENCE/SUMMARY/ SECRET.
(Erase heading not required.)

Instructions regarding War Diaries and Intelligence Summaries are contained in F.S. Regs., Part II. and the Staff Manual respectively. Title Pages will be prepared in manuscript.

Place	Date	Hour	Summary of Events and Information	Remarks and references to Appendices
STACEGHEM.	1.11.18.		HEADQUARTERS OF UNIT WERE AT STACEGHEM (Sheet 29.H.30.a.2.0.) Admitted sick - Other Ranks 20. Prevailing Disease, Influenza. MAJOR J.R. CRAIG, M.C., R.A.M.C., rejoined the Unit on completion of temporary duty in charge of detraining point at Sheet 28.L.13. The party detailed for temporary duty at the Civilian Hospital DU FORTE, COURTRAI, returned to duty with this Unit.	
"	2.11.18.		Admitted sick - Other Ranks 50. Prevailing Disease, Influenza. A sick post was opened by this Unit at VICHTE STATION.	
RECKEM.	3.11.18.		The Unit, less a holding party, proceeded to RECKEM (Sheet 28.R.23.c.6.4.) and Øpened a Divisional Rest Station at RECKEM CONVENT. Admitted sick - Officers 1, Other Ranks 31. Prevailing Disease, Influenza. CAPt. G. RAINFORD, R.A.M.C., transferred from the 94th Field Ambulance, reported for duty with this Unit. The Sick Post at VICHTE STATION was closed, and the holding party rejoined the Unit.	
"	4.11.18.		Admitted sick - Officers 2 including Brigadier-General SYMONS, C.M.G.,) Other Ranks 19. Prevailing Disease, Influenza. A.D.M.S., 31st Division inspected the Divisional Rest Station. MAJOR W. HUNT, M.C., R.A.M.C. reported for duty with this Unit on return from leave to the United Kingdom. The Sick Post at STACEGHEM was closed, and the holding party returned to the Unit.	
"	5.11.18.		Admitted sick - Officers 3, Other Ranks 52. Prevailing Disease, Influenza.	
"	6.11.18.		Admitted sick - Other Ranks 43. Prevailing Disease, Influenza. A.D.M.S., 31st Division, inspected the Divisional Rest Station.	
"	7.11.18.		Admitted - Wounded - Other Ranks 26. Sick - Other Ranks - 56. Prevailing Disease, Influenza.	

1875 Wt. W593/826 1,000,000 4/15 J.B.C. & A. A.D.S.S./Forms/C. 2118.

Army Form C. 2118

WAR DIARY
or
INTELLIGENCE/SUMMARY

(Erase heading not required.)

SECRET

(2)

Instructions regarding War Diaries and Intelligence Summaries are contained in F. S. Regs., Part II. and the Staff Manual respectively. Title Pages will be prepared in manuscript.

Place	Date	Hour	Summary of Events and Information	Remarks and references to Appendices
RECKEM.	7.11.18.		A.D.M.S., 31st Division, visited the Divisional Rest Station.	
"	8.11.18.		Admitted – Wounded – Other Ranks 2; Sick – Other Ranks 45. Prevailing Disease, Influenza. Major W. HUNT, M.C., R.A.M.C., proceeded for temporary duty with A.D.M.S., 31st Division. A Post was opened by this Unit at LAUWE for the treatment of Divisional sick.	
"	9.11.18.		Admitted – Wounded – Officers 1, Other Ranks 20. Died of Wounds – Other Ranks 1. Sick – Officers 1, Other Ranks 29. Prevailing Disease, Influenza.	
AVELGHEM.	10.11.18.		Admitted – Sick – Other Ranks 8. Prevailing Disease, Influenza. The Unit (less a holding party) moved to AVELGHEM (Sheet 29.P.34.c.4.8.) The Divisional Sick Post at LAUWE was closed, and the party rejoined this Unit. Lieut. N.B. PEACOCK, R.A.M.C., reported for temporary duty with 93rd and 94th Field Ambulance.	
"	11.11.18.		Admitted – Sick – Officers 1; Other Ranks 18. Prevailing Disease, Influenza. The Divisional Rest Station at RECKEM CONVENT was closed, and the party returned to the Unit.	
"	12.11.18.		Admitted – Sick – Other Ranks 1. Prevailing Disease, Influenza.	
"	13.11.18.		Capt. J.V. McNALLY, R.A.M.C., reported for duty with this Unit on transfer from the 93rd Field Ambulance.	
RECKEM.	14.11.18.		The Unit moved from AVELGHEM to RECKEM, and opened for the reception of sick at RECKEM CONVENT. A Sick Post was established at SWEVEGHEM.	
"	15.11.18.		Admitted – Sick – Other Ranks 9. Prevailing Disease, Influenza. The Sick Post was closed at SWEVEGHEM, and the party rejoined the Unit. Lieut. N.B. PEACOCK, R.A.M.C., returned to the Unit from temporary duty with the 94th Field Ambulance.	
"	16.11.18.		Admitted – Sick – Other Ranks 6. Prevailing Disease, Influenza.	

Army Form C. 2118.

WAR DIARY
or
INTELLIGENCE/SUMMARY.   SECRET.   (3)
(Erase heading not required.)

Instructions regarding War Diaries and Intelligence Summaries are contained in F. S. Regs., Part II. and the Staff Manual respectively. Title pages will be prepared in manuscript.

Place	Date	Hour	Summary of Events and Information	Remarks and references to Appendices
RECKEM.	16.11.18.		A.D.M.S., 31st Division, visited the Unit.	
"	17.11.18.		Admitted – Sick – Other Ranks 8. Prevailing Disease, Influenza. One other rank reinforcement was received. Lieut. J.A. SCHRAMM, M.C., U.S.A., reported for duty with this Unit on transfer from the 87th Field Ambulance.	
"	18.11.18.		Admitted – Sick – Other Ranks 7. Prevailing Disease, Influenza. The Unit paraded at MARCKE for the presentation of medal ribbons by the General Officer Commanding 31st Division. Lieut. E.J.S. BONNETT, R.A.M.C., rejoined the Unit on completion of temporary duty with 12th Battalion, Norfolk Regiment.	
"	19.11.18.		Admitted – Sick – Other Ranks 23. Prevailing Disease, Influenza, I.C.T. and Diarrhoea.	
"	20.11.18.		Admitted – Sick – Other Ranks 25. Prevailing Disease, Influenza and Diarrhoea. D.D.M.S., XIX Corps inspected the Divisional Rest Station. Lieut. E.J.S. BONNETT, R.A.M.C., proceeded to report for duty with the 31st Machine Gun Battn.	
"	21.11.18.		Admitted – Sick – Officers 1 (Lieut-Colonel J. SHERWOOD KELLY, V.C., C.M.G., D.S.O., Officer Commanding 12th Norfolk Regiment); Other Ranks 12. Prevailing Disease, Influenza.	
"	22.11.18.		A detachment of Officers, N.C.O's and men attended a parade in the Convent at MARCKE to meet the D.M.S., Second Army. MAJOR J.R. CRAIG, M.C., R.A.M.C., proceeded on seven days' leave to Paris from 24.11.18 to 1.12.18.	
"	24.11.18.		Admitted – Sick – Officers 2; Other Ranks 23. Prevailing Disease, Influenza.	
VLAMERTINGHE	25.11.18.		The Unit moved from RECKEM to VLAMERTINGHE (Sheet 28.H.3.a.1.8.)	

2353 Wt. W2544/1454 700,000 5/15 D.D.&L.   A.D.S.S./Forms/C. 2118.

Army Form C. 2118.

WAR DIARY
or
INTELLIGENCE/SUMMARY/   S E C R E T.   (4)
(Erase heading not required.)

Instructions regarding War Diaries and Intelligence Summaries are contained in F. S. Regs., Part II. and the Staff Manual respectively. Title pages will be prepared in manuscript.

Place	Date	Hour	Summary of Events and Information	Remarks and references to Appendices
VLAMERTINGHE.	25.11.18.		Admitted — Sick — Officers 2; Other Ranks 8. Prevailing Disease, Venereal. CONGRATULATION:— At the end of their march to-day, the Divisional Commander complimented the Unit on its fine marching.	
STEENVOORDE.	26.11.18.		The Unit moved from VLAMERTINGHE to STEENVOORDE (Sheet 27.K.31.c.) Admitted — Sick — Officer 1; Other Ranks 13. Prevailing Disease, Influenza.	
LE NIEPPE.	27.11.18.		The Unit moved from STEENVOORDE to LE NIEPPE (Sheet 27.T.11.a.) Admitted — Sick — Officers 2; Other Ranks 10. Prevailing Disease, Influenza. Lieut. J.A. SCHRAMM, M.C., U.S.A., reported for duty with the 24th Royal Welsh Fusiliers.	
St. MARTIN au LAERT.	28.11.18.		The Unit moved from LE NIEPPE to St. MARTIN au LAERT (St. Omer combined sheet R.32.b.) Admitted — Sick — Other Ranks 12. Prevailing Disease, Influenza.	
"	29.11.18.		Admitted — Sick — Other Ranks 8. Prevailing Disease, Influenza.	
"	30.11.18.		Admitted — Sick — Other Ranks 8. Prevailing Disease, Influenza. Officers admitted — Sick — 21; wounded 1. Officers evacuated — Sick — 21; wounded 1. Other Ranks admitted — Sick — 618. Other Ranks admitted — wounded — 40. Other Ranks evacuated — sick — 570. Other Ranks evacuated — wounded — 39. Other Ranks discharged to duty — sick — 48. Other Ranks died of wounds 1. The Unit remained at St. MARTIN au LAERT.	

Lieut-Colonel, R.A.M.C.,
Commanding 95th Field Ambulance.

95TH FIELD AMBULANCE.
Date 1.12.18.

No. 45 F.A.

COMMITTEE FOR THE
MEDICAL HISTORY OF THE WAR
6 MAR 1919
Date

WAR DIARY
or
INTELLIGENCE/SUMMARY

(Erase heading not required.)

Army Form C. 2118.

Place	Date	Hour	Summary of Events and Information	Remarks and references to Appendices
ST MARTIN au LAERT.	1.12.18.		HEADQUARTERS OF UNIT AT ST MARTIN au LAERT (St Omer Combined Sheet R.32.b)	
"	3.12.18.		MAJOR J.R. CRAIG, M.C., R.A.M.C., reported for duty on return from leave to PARIS.	
"	5.12.18.		CAPT. G. RAINFORD, R.A.M.C., reported for temporary duty with the 24th Bn. Royal Welsh Fusiliers, in relief of LIEUT. J.A. SCHRAMM, M.C., U.S.A., who returned to this Unit for duty.	
"	7.12.18.		LIEUT. J.A. SCHRAMM, M.C., U.S.A., was transferred for duty with No.80 Labour Group, LILLE.	
"	11.12.18.		A.D.M.S., 31st Division, visited this Unit.	
"	12.12.18.		LIEUT. J.A. SCHRAMM, M.C., U.S.A., was reported for duty with this Unit, and detailed for temporary duty with 93rd Field Ambulance.	
"	13.12.18.		CAPT. J.V. McNALLY, R.A.M.C., relieved CAPT. G. RAINFORD, R.A.M.C., in temporary medical charge of the 24th Bn. Royal Welsh Fusiliers.	
"	14.12.18.		CAPT. G. RAINFORD, R.A.M.C., proceeded on One Month Special Leave to the United Kingdom. Two N.C.O's and 23 men of this Unit proceeded to No.3 Canadian Stationary Hospital for temporary duty.	
LEULINGHEM.	17.12.18.		Unit removed from ST MARTIN au LAERT to LEULINGHEM (Sheet 27a.S.E. W.16.a.)	
"	21.12.18.		The undermentioned N.C.O's of this Unit were awarded the Croix de Guerre by the French authorities. French Croix de Guerre with Star - 34858 S.Sgt. H.J.D. PORTER, M.M. French Croix de Guerre Brigade - 69063 Sgt. J.H. JONES, M.M. (Authority 31st Division, C. 206/90/4.A., Dated 21.12.18.	

Army Form C. 2118.

WAR DIARY
or
INTELLIGENCE/ SUMMARY.
(Erase heading not required.)

Instructions regarding War Diaries and Intelligence Summaries are contained in F. S. Regs., Part II. and the Staff Manual respectively. Title pages will be prepared in manuscript.

Place	Date	Hour	Summary of Events and Information	Remarks and references to Appendices
LEULINGHEM.	24.12.18.		Admitted–Sick–Other Ranks 7. Prevailing Disease, Influenza.	
"	25.12.18.		Admitted–Sick–Other Ranks 2. Prevailing Disease Influenza. A.D.M.S., 31st Division, visited this Unit.	
"	26.12.18.		Admitted–Sick–Other Ranks 4. Prevailing Disease Influenza. LIEUT–COLONEL R.E. DRAKE–BROCKMAN, D.S.O., R.A.M.C, assumed duty as A.D.M.S., 31st Division, during the absence on leave of COLONEL F.J. BRAKENRIDGE, C.M.G., A.M.S.	
"	27.12.18.		Admitted–Sick–Other Ranks 2. Prevailing Disease Influenza.	
"	28.12.18		Admitted–Sick–Other Ranks–1 Prevailing Disease Influenza. Captain. J.V. McNALLY, R.A.M.C., was posted in Medical Charge of 24th. Bn. Royal Welsh Fusiliers, in relief of Captain. G.C. COSSAR, M.C., R.A.M.C., and was struck off the strength of this Unit from this date.	
"	29.12.18		Admitted–Sick–Other Ranks–8 Prevailing Disease Influenza.	
"	30.12.18		Admitted Sick–Other Ranks–10 Prevailing Disease. Influenza.	
WISQUES	31.12.18		Admitted–Sick–OtherRanks –9 Prevailing Disease German Measles. LIEUT. J.A. SCHRAMM., M.C., U.S.A., proceeded on 14 days' Leave to England 31.12.18 to 14.1.19. UNIT moved to WISQUES (Sheet HAZEBROUCK 5.A. 4.C.27.67.) and opened a Convalescent Hospital for 350 patients from troops in XIX Corps Area. TOTAL ADMISSIONS–OTHER RANKS –SICK–67 EVACUATIONS–OTHER RANKS– 56. DISCHARGED TO DUTY–OTHER RANKS– 3.	

LIEUT–COLONEL, R.A.M.C.
COMMANDING
35th FIELD AMBULANCE

31 DIV
Box 2131

No. 90 Field Ambulance

Jan 1919

WAR DIARY
or
INTELLIGENCE SUMMARY

(Erase heading not required.)

Army Form C. 2118

Instructions regarding War Diaries and Intelligence Summaries are contained in F.S. Regs., Part II. and the Staff Manual respectively. Title Pages will be prepared in manuscript.

Place	Date	Hour	Summary of Events and Information	Remarks and references to Appendices
WISQUES	1.1.19		HEADQUARTERS OF UNIT AT WISQUES (Sheet HAZEBROUCK 5a 4C 27.6W). 1 Other Ranks R. A. M. C. proceeded to ENGLAND for Demobilisation. Admitted-Transfers and Sick-Other Ranks-25	
"	2.1.19		Major J.R.CRAIG. M.C. R.A.M.C.proceeded to ENGLAND to report to Adastral House LONDON. 2 Other Ranks proceeded to ENGLAND for Demobilisation. Admitted-Transfers and Sick-Other Ranks-5.	
"	3.1.19		2 Other Ranks R.A.M.C. proceeded to ENGLAND for Demobilisation. Admitted-Transfers and Sick-1.	
"	4.1.19		MAJOR HUNT M.C. R.A.M.C. reported on relief from duties at A.D.M.S. Office 31st Division. 2 N.C.O,s and 25 Men returned from temporary duty with 3 CANADIAN STATIONARY HOSPITAL MALASSESE. ST OMER. Admitted- Transfers and Sick-3.	
"	5.1.19		LIEUT E.J.S.BONNETT R. A. M. C. reported for duty from 31st M. G. Batt. Admitted-Transfers and Sick-24.	
"	6.1.19		2 Other Ranks R. A. M. C. proceeded to ENGLAND for Demobilisation. Admitted-Transfers and Sick-17.	
"	7.1.19		LIEUT F. L. RIGBY reported for duty from 12th R. S. F. 31st Division. No 68768 PTE J. ATKINSON R.A.M.C. awarded the Croix de Guerre by the BELGIAN Authorities-Auth 2nd Corps -wire-D211 of 7.1.19. Admitted-Transfers and Sick-16.	
"	8.1.19		Admitted-Transfers and Sick-15.	
"	9.1.19		4 Other Ranks R.A.M.C. reported to 3 CANADIAN STATIONARY HOSPITAL for Special temporary duty.	

Army Form C. 2118

WAR DIARY
or
INTELLIGENCE SUMMARY

(Erase heading not required.)

Instructions regarding War Diaries and Intelligence Summaries are contained in F.S. Regs., Part II and the Staff Manual respectively. Title Pages will be prepared in manuscript.

Place	Date	Hour	Summary of Events and Information	Remarks and references to Appendices
WISQUES.	9.1.19		(con) 1 Other Ranks R.A.M.C. and 1 Other Ranks R.A.S.C. proceeded to ENGLAND for Demobilisation. Admitted–Transfers and Sick–Other Ranks–1.	C.E.M.
"	10.1.19		Lieut Col R.E. DRAKE-BROCKMAN. D.S.O. R.A.M.C. proceeded on one months Special Leave to the U.K. MAJOR W. HUNT. M.C. R.A.M.C. assumed command of Unit. 1 Other Ranks R.A.M.C. proceeded to ENGLAND for Demobilisation. Admitted–Transfers and Sick–Other Ranks–11.	C.E.M.
"	11.1.19		Admitted–Transfers and Sick–Other Ranks–4.	C.E.M.
"	12.1.19		5 Other Ranks R.A.M.C. proceeded to ENGLAND for Demobilisation. Admitted–Transfers and Sick–Other Ranks– 2.	C.E.M.
"	13.1.19		A/D.D.M.S. ST OMER XIX CORPS visited and inspected the Camp. Admitted–Transfers and Sick– Other Ranks–2.	C.E.M.
"	14.1.19		Admitted–Transfers and Sick–Other Ranks–5.	C.E.M.
"	15.1.19		CAPTN G. RAINFORD. R.A.M.C. reported for duty on expiration of leave to U.K. Admitted–Transfers and Sick–Other Ranks–6.	C.E.M.
"	16.1.19		Admitted–Transfers and Sick–Other Ranks–5. Prevailing Disease P.U.O.	C.E.M.
"	17.1.19		Admitted–Transfers and Sick–Other Ranks–12.	C.E.M.
"	18.1.19		A/A.D.M.S. ST OMER. XIX CORPS visited and inspected the Camp. LIEUT J.A. SCHRAMM M.C. U.S.A. reported to 93rd Field Ambulance for temporary duty on expiration of Leave to U.K. 2 Other Ranks R.A.M.C. proceeded to ENGLAND for Demobilisation. Admitted–Transfers and Sick–Other Ranks–7. Prevailing Disease–Scabies.	C.E.M.

Army Form C. 2118

WAR DIARY
or
INTELLIGENCE SUMMARY

(Erase heading not required)

Instructions regarding War Diaries and Intelligence
Summaries are contained in F. S. Regs., Part II.
and the Staff Manual respectively. Title Pages
will be prepared in manuscript.

Place	Date	Hour	Summary of Events and Information	Remarks and references to Appendices
WISQUES	19.1.19		LIEUT E.J.S.BONNETT R.A.M.C.proceeded to XIX CORPS CONCENTRATION CAMP HAZEBROUCK for temporary duty in relief of CAPTN C.E.MERYON R.A.M.C.who reported to this Unit for duty. 5 Other Ranks R.A.M.C. proceeded to ENGLAND for Demobilisation. Admitted-Transfers and Sick-Other Ranks-5.	cdh.
"	20.1.19		2 Other Ranks R.A.M.C. proceeded to ENGLAND for Demobilisation. Admitted Transfers and Sick-Other Ranks-9.	cdh.
"	21.1.19		8 Other Ranks R.A.M.C. proceeded to ENGLAND for Demobilisation. Admitted-Transfers and Sick-Other Ranks-10- Prevailing Disease-Scabies.	cdh.
"	22.1.19		2 Other Ranks R.A.M.C. proceeded to ENGLAND for Demobilisation. Admitted-Transfers and Sick-Other Ranks-8.	cdh.
"	23.1.19		Admitted Transfers and Sick-Officers -1-Other Ranks-4. Capt. G. RAINFORD R.A.M.C.proceeded to XIX CORPS CONCENTRATION CAMP for temporary duty in relief of LIEUT. E.J.S. BONNETT)	cdh.
"	24.1.19		LIEUT E.J.S.BONNETT R.A.M.C. proceeded on 10days Special Leave to ROUEN. (LIEUT. E.J.S. BONNETT) Admitted-Transfers and Sick-Other Ranks-7.	cdh.
"	25.1.19		D.A.D.M.S. 31st DIVISION visited the Camp. No 68898 Q.M.S.PRIME B.H. R.A.M.C. awarded the Meritorious Service Medal Auth:- London Gazette Supplement dated 18.1.1919. Admitted-Transfers and Sick-Other Ranks-2.	cdh.
"	26.1.19		Admitted-Transfers and Sick-Other Ranks-7.Prevailing Disease P.U.O.	cdh.
"	27.1.19		A.D.M.S. 31st Division visited the Camp. MAJOR W.HUNT.M.C. R.A.M.C. proceeded to ENGLAND to report to M.S.I. COLONIAL. WAR OFFICE. CAPTN C.E. MERYON R.A.M.C. assumed command of Unit during temporary absence of Lieut Col R. E. DRAKE-BROCKMAN D.S.O. R.A.M.C. on leave. Admitted-Transfers and Sick-Other Ranks-3. Prevailing Disease I.C.T.	cdh.

Army Form C. 2118

WAR DIARY
or
INTELLIGENCE SUMMARY

(Erase heading not required.)

Instructions regarding War Diaries and Intelligence Summaries are contained in F. S. Regs., Part II. and the Staff Manual respectively. Title Pages will be prepared in manuscript.

Place	Date	Hour	Summary of Events and Information	Remarks and references to Appendices
WISQUES	28.1.19.		Admitted-Transfers and Sick-Other Ranks-4.	C&M
"	29.1.19		BRIGADE GENERAL AND STAFF CAPTAIN of 94th INFANTRY BRIGADE 31st DIVISION visited the Camp. LIEUT F. L. RIGBY R.A.M.C. proceeded to 12th R.S.F. 31st Division as Medical Officer i/c. LIEUT J.A.SCHRAMM M.C. R.A.M.C. U.S.A. reported for duty from 93rd Field Ambulance. 1 Officer and 10 Other Ranks R.A.M.C. awarded the Divisional Badge and Parchment for valuable services rendered with the Unit Auth:- A.D.M.S. C 121 dated 28.1.19. 1 N.C.O. and 6 Other Ranks R.A.M.C. proceeded to 93rd Field Ambulance for Temporary duty. Admitted-Transfers and Sick- Other Ranks-4.	C&M C&M
"	30.1.19		Admitted-Transfers and Sick-Other Ranks-22	C&M
"	31.1.19.		Admitted-Sick and Transfers-Other Ranks-3.	C&M

LIEUT.-COLONEL R.A.M.C.,
COMMANDING
95th FIELD AMBULANCE

160/3501

95. H.A.

Jan 1919

Army Form C. 2118.

WAR DIARY
or
INTELLIGENCE SUMMARY.

(Erase heading not required.)

Instructions regarding War Diaries and Intelligence Summaries are contained in F. S. Regs., Part II. and the Staff Manual respectively. Title pages will be prepared in manuscript.

95 4n Cent 1/61 37

Place	Date	Hour	Summary of Events and Information	Remarks and references to Appendices
WISQUES	1.1.19		HEADQUARTERS OF UNIT AT WISQUES (Sheet HAZEBROUCK 5a 4C 27.6U). 1 Other Ranks R. A. M. C. proceeded to ENGLAND for Demobilisation. Admitted Transfers and Sick-Other Ranks-35	CEM
"	2.1.19		Major J.R.CRAIG. M.C. R.A.M.C.proceeded to ENGLAND to report to Adastral House LONDON. 2 Other Ranks proceeded to ENGLAND for Demobilisation. Admitted Transfers and Sick-Other Ranks-5.	CEM
"	3.1.19		2 Other Ranks R.A.M.C. proceeded to ENGLAND for Demobilisation. Admitted-Transfers and Sick-1.	1/37
"	4.1.19		MAJOR HUNT M.C. R.A.M.C. reported on relief from duties at A.D.M.S. Office 31st Division. 3 N.C.O.s and 23 Men returned from temporary duty with 3 CANADIAN STATIONARY HOSPITAL MALASSISE. ST OMER. Admitted-Transfers and Sick-3.	CEM
"	5.1.19		LIEUT E.J.S.BONNETT R. A. M. C. reported for duty from 31st M. G. Batt. Admitted-Transfers and Sick-24.	CEM
"	6.1.19		3 Other Ranks R. A. M. C. proceeded to ENGLAND for Demobilisation. Admitted-Transfers and Sick-17.	CEM
"	7.1.19		LIEUT F. L. RIGBY reported for duty from 12th R. S. F. 31st Division. No 68768 PTE J. ATKINSON R.A.M.C. awarded the Croix de Guerre by the BELGIAN Authorities- Auth and Corps -wire-D211 of 7.1.19. Admitted-Transfers and Sick-16.	CEM
"	8.1.19		Admitted-Transfers and Sick-15.	CEM
"	9.1.19		4 Other Ranks R.A.M.C. reported to 3 CANADIAN STATIONARY HOSPITAL for Special temporary duty.	1/37

2353 Wt. W2514/1454 700,000 5/15 D.D.&L. A.D.S.S./Forms/C. 2118.

Army Form C. 2118

WAR DIARY
or
INTELLIGENCE/SUMMARY
(Erase heading not required.)

Instructions regarding War Diaries and Intelligence Summaries are contained in F. S. Regs., Part II. and the Staff Manual respectively. Title Pages will be prepared in manuscript.

Place	Date	Hour	Summary of Events and Information	Remarks and references to Appendices
WISQUES.	9.1.19 (con)		1 Other Ranks R.A.M.C. and 1 Other Ranks R.A.S.C. proceeded to ENGLAND for Demobilisation. Admitted—Transfers and Sick—Other Ranks—1.	CSM.
"	10.1.19		Lieut Col R.E. DRAKE-BROCKMAN. D.S.O. R.A.M.C. proceeded on one months Special Leave to the U.K. MAJOR W. HUNT. M.C. R.A.M.C. assumed command of Unit. 1 Other Ranks R.A.M.C. proceeded to ENGLAND for Demobilisation. Admitted—Transfers and Sick—Other Ranks—11.	CSM.
"	11.1.19		Admitted—Transfers and Sick—Other Ranks—4.	CSM.
"	12.1.19		5 Other Ranks R.A.M.C. proceeded to ENGLAND for Demobilisation. Admitted—Transfers and Sick—Other Ranks—2.	CSM.
"	13.1.19		A/D.M.S. ST OMER XIX CORPS visited and inspected the Camp. Admitted—Transfers and Sick—Other Ranks—2.	CSM.
"	14.1.19		Admitted—Transfers and Sick—Other Ranks—5.	CSM.
"	15.1.19		CAPTN G. RAINFORD. R.A.M.C. reported for duty on expiration of leave to U.K. Admitted—Transfers and Sick—Other Ranks—6.	CSM.
"	16.1.19		Admitted—Transfers and Sick—Other Ranks—5. Prevailing Disease P.U.O.	CSM.
"	17.1.19		Admitted—Transfers and Sick—Other Ranks—12.	CSM.
"	18.1.19		A/A.D.M.S. ST OMER. XIX CORPS visited and inspected the Camp. LIEUT J.A. SCIRMER M.C. U.S.A. reported to 63rd Field Ambulance for temporary duty on expiration of leave to U.K. 3 Other Ranks R.A.M.C. proceeded to ENGLAND for Demobilisation. Admitted—Transfers and Sick—Other Ranks—7. Prevailing Disease—Scabies.	CSM.

Army Form C. 2118

WAR DIARY
or
INTELLIGENCE SUMMARY

(Erase heading not required.)

Instructions regarding War Diaries and Intelligence Summaries are contained in F. S. Regs., Part II. and the Staff Manual respectively. Title Pages will be prepared in manuscript.

Place	Date	Hour	Summary of Events and Information	Remarks and references to Appendices
WISQUES	19.1.19		LIEUT E.J.S. BONNETT R.A.M.C. proceeded to XIX CORPS CONCENTRATION CAMP HAZEBROUCK for temporary duty in relief of CAPTN C.E. MERYON R.A.M.C. who reported to this Unit for duty. 5 Other Ranks R.A.M.C. proceeded to ENGLAND for Demobilisation. Admitted-Transfers and Sick-Other Ranks-5.	CSM
"	20.1.19		2 Other Ranks R.A.M.C. proceeded to ENGLAND for Demobilisation. Admitted-Transfers and Sick-Other Ranks-9.	CSM
"	21.1.19		2 Other Ranks R.A.M.C. proceeded to ENGLAND for Demobilisation. Admitted-Transfers and Sick-Other Ranks-10. Prevailing Disease-Scabies.	CSM
"	22.1.19		2 Other Ranks R.A.M.C. proceeded to ENGLAND for Demobilisation. Admitted-Transfers and Sick-Other Ranks-8.	CSM
"	23.1.19		Admitted-Transfers and Sick-Officers -1-Other Ranks-4. CAPT. G. RAINFORD R.A.M.C. Proceeded to XIX CORPS CONCENTRATION CAMP FOR TEMP. DUTY in relief of LIEUT E.J.S.BONNETT. R.A.M.C. proceeded on 10days Special Leave to ROUEN. (LIEUT. E.J.S.BONNETT)	CSM
"	24.1.19		Admitted-Transfers and Sick-Other Ranks-7.	CSM
"	25.1.19		D.A.D.M.S. 51st DIVISION visited the Camp. No 68898 Q.M.S.PRIME B.H. R.A.M.C. awarded the Meritorious Service Medal Auth:- London Gazette Supplement dated 18.1.1919. Admitted-Transfers and Sick-Other Ranks-3.	CSM
"	26.1.19		Admitted-Transfers and Sick-Other Ranks-7.Prevailing Disease P.U.O.	CSM
"	27.1.19		A.D.M.S. 31st Division visited the Camp. MAJOR W.HUNT.M.C. R.A.M.C. proceeded to ENGLAND to report to M.S.I. COLONIAL. WAR OFFICE. CAPTN C.E. MERYON R.A.M.C. assumed command of Unit during temporary absence of Lieut Col R. E. DRAKE-BROCKMAN D.S.O. R.A.M.C. on leave. Prevailing Disease I.C.T.	CSM

Army Form C. 2118

WAR DIARY
or
INTELLIGENCE SUMMARY

Instructions regarding War Diaries and Intelligence Summaries are contained in F. S. Regs., Part II. and the Staff Manual respectively. Title Pages will be prepared in manuscript.

Place	Date	Hour	Summary of Events and Information	Remarks and references to Appendices
WISQUES	28.1.19.		Admitted—Transfers and Sick—Other Ranks—4.	C34
"	29.1.19		BRIGADE GENERAL AND STAFF CAPTAIN of 94th INFANTRY BRIGADE 51st DIVISION visited the Camp. LIEUT F. L. RIGBY R.A.M.C. proceeded to 12th R.S.F. 31st Division as Medical Officer i/c. LIEUT J.A.SCHRAMM M.C. A.A.M.C. U.S.A. reported for duty from 93rd Field Ambulance. 1 Officer and 10 Other Ranks R.A.M.C. awarded the Divisional Badge and Parchment for valuable services rendered with the Unit Auth:- A.D.M.S. C 121 dated 28.1.19. 1 N.C.O. and 6 Other Ranks R.A.M.C. proceeded to 95rd Field Ambulance for Temporary duty. Admitted—Transfers and Sick— Other Ranks—4.	C34
"	30.1.19		Admitted—Transfers and Sick—Other Ranks—22	C34
"	31.1.19.		Admitted—Sick and Transfers—Other Ranks—3.	C34

95TH FIELD AMBULANCE.
No..................
Date.................

C R Morgan Capt
for
LIEUT.-COLONEL R.A.M.C.,
COMMANDING
95th FIELD AMBULANCE.

No. 95 Field Ambulance

Army Form C. 2118

WAR DIARY
or
INTELLIGENCE SUMMARY

(Erase heading not required.)

Instructions regarding War Diaries and Intelligence Summaries are contained in F.S. Regs., Part II. and the Staff Manual respectively. Title Pages will be prepared in manuscript.

Place	Date	Hour	Summary of Events and Information	Remarks and references to Appendices
WISQUES	1.2.19.		HEADQUARTERS OF UNIT AT WISQUES (Sheet HAZEBROUCK 5a 4C 37. 67.) LIEUT N.B. PEACOCK, R.A.M.C., proceeded for temporary Medical Duty with 82nd LABOUR GROUP. LIEUT F.L. RIGBY, R.A.M.C. reported for duty from 12th ROYAL SCOTS FUSILIERS. Admitted Transfers and Sick-Other Ranks—4.	
"	2.2.19.		LIEUT J.A. SCHRAMM, M.C., U.S.A., proceeded for medical duty with 30th LABOUR GROUP, HAZEBROUCK. LIEUT E.J.S. BONNETT, R.A.M.C., returned from leave to ROUEN. Admitted Transfers and Sick-Other Ranks – 1.	
"	3.2.19.		Admitted Transfers and Sick-Other Ranks – 3.	
"	4.2.19.		CAPT & Q.MR. W. WILSON, R.A.M.C., proceeded on 14 days Special Leave to ENGLAND. Admitted Transfers and Sick-Other Ranks – 17.	
"	5.2.19.		Admitted Transfers and Sick-Other Ranks – 2.	
"	6.2.19.		Admitted Transfers and Sick-Other Ranks – 9.	
"	7.2.19.		A.D.M.S., 31st DIVISION visited the Camp. LIEUT E.J.S. BONNETT, R.A.M.C., proceeded on 14 days Special Leave to UNITED KINGDOM. 1 Other Ranks, R.A.M.C., and 1 Other Ranks "P.B." Batman attached R.A.S.C. proceeded to ENGLAND for demobilisation. Admitted Transfers and Sick-Other Ranks – 15.	
"	8.2.19.		3 Other Ranks, R.A.M.C., proceeded to ENGLAND for demobilisation. Admitted Transfers and Sick-Other Ranks – 13.	
"	9.2.19.		CAPT R.M. MC. MINN, R.A.M.C. reported for duty from 12th K.O.Y.L.I. 1 Other Ranks R.A.M.C., proceeded to ENGLAND for demobilisation.	

Army Form C. 2118

WAR DIARY
or
INTELLIGENCE SUMMARY
(Erase heading not required.)

Instructions regarding War Diaries and Intelligence Summaries are contained in F. S. Regs., Part II. and the Staff Manual respectively. Title Pages will be prepared in manuscript.

Place	Date	Hour	Summary of Events and Information	Remarks and references to Appendices
WISQUES	10.2.19.		LIEUT COL. R.E. DRAKE-BROCKMAN, D.S.O., R.A.M.C., reported for duty on expiration of leave to UNITED KINGDOM. Admitted Transfers and Sick-Other Ranks - 12.	
"	11.2.19.		1 Other Ranks, R.A.M.C., proceeded to ENGLAND for demobilisation. Admitted Transfers and Sick-Other Ranks - 4.	
"	12.2.19.		2 Other Ranks, R.A.M.C., proceeded to ENGLAND for demobilisation. Admitted Transfers and Sick-Other Ranks - 26.	
"	13.2.19.		1 Other Ranks, R.A.M.C., and 1 Other Ranks "P.B". Batman attached R.A.S.C., proceeded to ENGLAND for demobilisation. Admitted Transfers and Sick-Other Ranks - 9.	
"	14.2.19.		1 Other Ranks, R.A.M.C., proceeded to ENGLAND for demobilisation. Admitted Transfers and Sick-Other Ranks - 2.	
"	15.2.19.		D.D.M.S., 19TH CORPS visited and inspected this Camp. Admitted Transfers and Sick-Other Ranks - 14.	
"	16.2.19.		LIEUT N.B. PEACOCK, R.A.M.C., reported for duty from 82ND LABOUR GROUP. 1 Other Ranks, R.A.M.C., proceeded to ENGLAND for demobilisation. Admitted Transfers and Sick-Other Ranks - 2.	
"	17.2.19.		LIEUT J.A. SCHRAMM, M.C., U.S.A., posted in permanent Medical Charge of 30TH LABOUR GROUP and is struck off strength. 1 Other Ranks, R.A.M.C., proceeded to ENGLAND for demobilisation. Admitted Transfers and Sick-Other Ranks - 10.	

Army Form C. 2118

WAR DIARY
or
INTELLIGENCE SUMMARY
(Erase heading not required.)

Instructions regarding War Diaries and Intelligence Summaries are contained in F. S. Regs., Part II. and the Staff Manual respectively. Title Pages will be prepared in manuscript.

Place	Date	Hour	Summary of Events and Information	Remarks and references to Appendices
WISQUES	18.2.19.		Admitted Transfers and Sick-Other Ranks - 11.	
"	19.2.19.		2 Other Ranks, R.A.M.C., proceeded to ENGLAND for demobilisation. Admitted Transfers and Sick-Other Ranks - 10.	
"	20.2.19.		LIEUT N.B. PEACOCK, R.A.M.C., proceeded to 94TH FIELD AMBULANCE for temporary duty. CAPT & Q.MR. W. WILSON, R.A.M.C., reported for duty from leave to UNITED KINGDOM. 2 Other Ranks, R.A.M.C., and 1 "P.B." Batman attached R.A.S.C., proceeded to ENGLAND for demobilisation. Admitted Transfers and Sick-Other Ranks - 1.	
"	21.2.19.		Admitted Transfers and Sick-Other Ranks - 9.	
"	22.2.19.		2 Other Ranks, R.A.M.C., and 1"P.B." Batman attached R.A.S.C., proceeded to ENGLAND for demobilisation. Admitted Transfers and Sick-Other Ranks - 17.	
"	23.2.19.		CAPT & Q.MR. W. WILSON, R.A.M.C., proceeded for duty with D.A.G. 3RD ECHELON, and is struck off strength. LIEUT E.J.S. BONNETT, R.A.M.C., reported for duty from leave to UNITED KINGDOM. 1 R.A.S.C. Driver proceeded to ENGLAND for demobilisation. Admitted Transfers and Sick-Other Ranks - 2.	
"	24.2.19.		Admitted Transfers and Sick-Other Ranks - 7.	
"	25.2.19.		LIEUT F.L. RIGBY, R.A.M.C., proceeded on 14 days Special Leave to UNITED KINGDOM. LIEUT N.B. PEACOCK, R.A.M.C., proceeded on 14 days Special Leave to UNITED KINGDOM. 1 Other Ranks, R.A.M.C., proceeded to ENGLAND for demobilisation. Admitted Transfers and Sick-Other Ranks - 9.	

1875 Wt. W593/826 1,000,000 4/15 J.B.C. & A. A.D.S.S./Forms/C.2118.

Army Form C. 2118

WAR DIARY
or
INTELLIGENCE SUMMARY

(Erase heading not required.)

Instructions regarding War Diaries and Intelligence Summaries are contained in F. S. Regs., Part II. and the Staff Manual respectively. Title Pages will be prepared in manuscript.

Place	Date	Hour	Summary of Events and Information	Remarks and references to Appendices
WISQUES	26.2.19.		LIEUT E.J.S. BONNETT, R.A.M.C., proceeded to 94TH FIELD AMBULANCE for duty. 2 Other Ranks, R.A.M.C., proceeded to ENGLAND for demobilisation. Admitted Transfers and Sick-Other Ranks - 34.	
"	27.2.19.		3 Other Ranks, R.A.M.C., proceeded to ENGLAND for demobilisation. Admitted Transfers and Sick-Other Ranks - 3.	
"	28.2.19.		2 Other Ranks, R.A.M.C., proceeded to ENGLAND for demobilisation. Admitted Transfers and Sick-Other Ranks - 12. D.A.D.O.S., 31st Division, visited and inspected the Camp.	

LIEUT.-COLONEL R.A.M.S.,
COMMANDING
95th FIELD AMBULANCE.

95TH FIELD AMBULANCE.
No ....
Date 28.2.19.

140/3630

27 JUL 1919

25-4-7-9.

April 1919

Army Form C. 2118

WAR DIARY
or
INTELLIGENCE SUMMARY

(Erase heading not required.)

95 Fd Amb
VIII 38

Instructions regarding War Diaries and Intelligence Summaries are contained in F. S. Regs., Part II. and the Staff Manual respectively. Title Pages will be prepared in manuscript.

Place	Date	Hour	Summary of Events and Information	Remarks and references to Appendices
MALASISE	1.4.19.		HEADQUARTERS OF UNIT AT MALASISE (SH/27/X.17.D.) 1 Other Ranks, R.A.M.C., transferred (under escort) to No.10 STATIONARY HOSPITAL for duty. Admitted Transfers and Sick Other Ranks – 7.	c/M.
"	2.4.19.		CAPT. J.S.W.LEECH, R.A.M.C., transferred from No. 4 STATIONARY HOSPITAL. Admitted Transfers and Sick Other Ranks – 5.	c/M.
"	3.4.19.		Admitted Transfers and Sick Other Ranks – 2. Officers – 1. 1 Other Ranks, R.A.M.C., charged "whilst on Active Service, Desertion". Remanded for F.G.C.M	c/M.
"	4.4.19.		Admitted Transfers and Sick Other Ranks – 7.	c/M.
"	5.4.19.		Admitted Transfers and Sick Other Ranks – 2.	c/M.
"	6.4.19.		CAPT. J.S.W.LEECH, R.A.M.C., transferred to No. 4 STATIONARY HOSPITAL for duty. (Auth. A.D.M.S., 51st Division, M1714/144/1 d/6.4.19.). CAPT. G.D.FAIRLEY, R.A.M.C., transferred for duty from 93RD FIELD AMBULANCE (Auth. 51st. Division, R.A.M.C. Orders No.814 d/6.4.19). Admitted Transfers and Sick Other Ranks – 5.	c/M.
"	7.4.19.		CAPT. F.L.RIGBY, R.A.M.C., proceeded to ENGLAND for demobilisation. Admitted Transfers and Sick Other Ranks – 4.	c/M.
"	8.4.19.		Admitted Transfers and Sick Other Ranks – 2. German P.O.W.– 1.	c/M.

95TH FIELD AMBULANCE.

Army Form C. 2118

WAR DIARY
or
INTELLIGENCE SUMMARY
(Erase heading not required.)

Instructions regarding War Diaries and Intelligence Summaries are contained in F.S. Regs., Part II. and the Staff Manual respectively. Title Pages will be prepared in manuscript.

Place	Date	Hour	Summary of Events and Information	Remarks and references to Appendices
MALASISE	9.4.19.		Admitted Transfers and Sick Other Ranks - 3.	C.H.
"	10.4.19.		2 Other Ranks, R.A.S.C., M.T., transferred to 31st Division M.T. Column for duty. 2 DAIMLER AMBULANCES transferred to NO.9 VEHICLE RECEPTION PARK, ROUBAIX. 1 Other Ranks, R.A.M.C., transferred for duty with A.D.M.S. 5TH AREA. Admitted Transfers and Sick Other Ranks - 5.	C.H.
"	11.4.19.		No.T3/029354. S.S.M. HARRIS, G., R.A.S.C., H.T., proceeded on 14 days Leave to the UNITED KINGDOM. Admitted Transfers and Sick Other Ranks - 2.	C.H.
"	12.4.19.		1 Other Ranks, R.A.M.C., charged, whilst on Active Service, absent without Leave from 5.1.19. until apprehended at HINCHLEY on 5.3.19. Sentence 7 days F.P. No.2. Admitted Transfers and Sick Other Ranks - 1.	C.H.
"	13.4.19.		Admitted Transfers and Sick Other Ranks - Nil. - German P.O.W. - 3.	C.H.
"	14.4.19.		Admitted Transfers and Sick Other Ranks - Nil. German P.O.W. - 4.	C.H.
"	15.4.19.		Admitted Transfers and Sick Other Ranks - Nil.	C.H.
"	16.4.19.		Admitted Transfers and Sick Other Ranks - 3.	C.H.
"	17.4.19.		CAPT. G.D.FAIRLEY, R.A.M.C., proceeded for duty with 39 STATIONARY HOSPITAL. Admitted Transfers and Sick Other Ranks - 4.	C.H.
"	18.4.19.		Admitted Transfers and Sick Other Ranks - 1. German P.O.W. - 2.	C.H.

95TH FIELD AMBULANCE

Army Form C. 2118

WAR DIARY
or
INTELLIGENCE SUMMARY

(Erase heading not required.)

Instructions regarding War Diaries and Intelligence Summaries are contained in F. S. Regs., Part II. and the Staff Manual respectively. Title Pages will be prepared in manuscript.

95TH FIELD AMBULANCE.

No............
Date...........

Place	Date	Hour	Summary of Events and Information	Remarks and references to Appendices
MALASISE	19.4.19.		Admitted Transfers and Sick Other Ranks - 2.	c/H.
"	20.4.19.		Admitted Transfers and Sick Other Ranks - 1.	c/H.
"	21.4.19.		Admitted Transfers and Sick Other Ranks - 3.	c/H.
"	22.4.19.		Admitted Transfers and Sick Other Ranks - 5.	c/H.
"	23.4.19.		Admitted Transfers and Sick Other Ranks - 2.	c/H.
"	24.4.19.		Admitted Transfers and Sick Other Ranks - Nil.	c/H.
"	25.4.19.		Admitted Transfers and Sick Other Ranks - 1.	c/H.
"	26.4.19.		Admitted Transfers and Sick Other Ranks - Nil.	c/H.
"	27.4.19.		Admitted Transfers and Sick Other Ranks - Nil.	c/H.
"	28.4.19.		Admitted Transfers and Sick Other Ranks - 2.	c/H.
"	29.4.19.		Admitted Transfers and Sick Other Ranks - 3.	c/H.
"	30.4.19.		Admitted Transfers and Sick Other Ranks - 3.	c/H.

MAJOR, R.A.M.C.
COMMANDING
95th FIELD AMBULANCE

Army Form C. 2118

95 th Army

Vol 39

WAR DIARY
or
INTELLIGENCE SUMMARY

(Erase heading not required.)

Instructions regarding War Diaries and Intelligence Summaries are contained in F. S. Regs., Part II. and the Staff Manual respectively. Title Pages will be prepared in manuscript.

Place	Date	Hour	Summary of Events and Information	Remarks and references to Appendices
MALASISE.	1/5/19.		Headquarters of Unit at Malasise (Sh/27/X.17.D.) Admitted Transfers and sick other Ranks - nil.	CRM.
"	2/5/19.		Admitted Transfers and sick other Ranks - nil. T/Captain C.E. Meyer, RAMC relinquishes his acting rank of Major.	CRM
"	3/5/19.		Admitted Transfers and sick other Ranks - nil. 2 Other Ranks, RAMC, evacuated sick to No. 4 Stationary Hospital.	CRM
"	4/5/19.		Admitted Transfers and sick other Ranks - nil.	CRM
"	5/5/19.		Staff Sgt. Major Harris, G. RAMC HT, proceeds to 287 (H.T.) Co. R.A.S.C., for duty.	CRM
"	6/5/19.		Admitted Transfers and sick other Ranks - nil. 1 Other Rank, RAMC, transferred to R.A.M.C. 5th Area. Hospital (XIX Corps Convalescent Camp) closed down, under instructions received from A.D.M.S. 5th Area. Cases not fit for duty transferred to No. 4 Stationary Hospital.	CRM
"	7/5/19.		nil.	CRM
"95TH FIELD AMBULANCE	8/5/19.		nil.	CRM

Army Form C. 2118

WAR DIARY
or
INTELLIGENCE SUMMARY
(Erase heading not required.)

Instructions regarding War Diaries and Intelligence Summaries are contained in F. S. Regs., Part II. and the Staff Manual respectively. Title Pages will be prepared in manuscript.

Place	Date	Hour	Summary of Events and Information	Remarks and references to Appendices
MARSEILLES	9/5/19.		6 Other Ranks R.A.M.C. proceeded to England for demobilisation.	Copy.
"	10/5/19.		nil.	Copy.
"	11/5/19.		"	Copy.
"	12/5/19.		"	Copy.
"	13/5/19.		"	Copy.
"	14/5/19.		2 R.A.S.C., M.T. Drivers transferred to 94th Field Ambulance.	Copy.
"	15/5/19.		nil.	Copy.
"	16/5/19.		Medical Equipment and Stores returned to 31 Advance Depot of Medical Stores, till further instructions from A.D.M.S. 3rd Area.	Copy.
"	17/5/19.		"	Copy.
95TH FIELD AMBULANCE	18/5/19.		3 O.R. (R.A.S.C., M.T.) proceeded to England for demobilisation.	Copy.
	19/5/19.		nil.	Copy.

WAR DIARY
or
INTELLIGENCE SUMMARY

Army Form C. 2118

Place	Date	Hour	Summary of Events and Information	Remarks and references to Appendices
MARSEILLE	9/5/19		6 Other Ranks R.A.M.C. proceeded to England for demobilisation.	CRM
"	10/5/19		vie.	CRM
"	11/5/19		"	CRM
"	12/5/19		"	CRM
"	13/5/19		"	CRM
"	14/5/19		2 R.A.S.C. H.T. Drivers transferred to 94th Field Ambulance.	CRM
"	15/5/19		vie.	CRM
"	16/5/19		Medical Equipment and Stores returned to 31 Advanced Depot of Medical Stores till further instructions from A.D.M.S. 3rd Area.	CRM
"	17/5/19		"	CRM
95TH FIELD AMBULANCE	18/5/19		3 O.R. (R.A.S.C. M.T.) proceeded to England for demobilisation.	CRM
	19/5/19		vie.	CRM

WAR DIARY or INTELLIGENCE SUMMARY

Army Form C. 2118

95 Lt Amb — Vol 39

Place	Date	Hour	Summary of Events and Information	Remarks and references to Appendices
MALASISE.	1/5/19		Headquarters of Unit at Malasise (Sh/27/X.17.D.) Admitted Transfers and Sick Other Ranks - Nil.	C.R.M.
"	2/5/19		Admitted Transfers and Sick Other Ranks - Nil. T/Captain C.E. Weyer, R.A.M.C. relinquishes the acting rank of Major.	C.R.M.
"	3/5/19		Admitted Transfers and Sick Other Ranks - Nil. 2 Other Ranks, R.A.M.C. evacuated Sick to No. 4 Stationary Hospital.	C.R.M.
"	4/5/19		Admitted Transfers and Sick Other Ranks - Nil.	C.R.M.
"	5/5/19		Staff Sgt. Major Harris. G. R.A.M.C. H.T. proceeded to 287 (H.T.) Co. A.A.S.C. for duty. Admitted Transfers and Sick Other Ranks - Nil. 1 Other Rank, R.A.M.C. transferred to R.R.M.S. 5th Area.	C.R.M.
"	6/5/19		Hospital (x1x Corps Convcts and Camp) closed down, under instructions received from D.D.M.S. 5th Area. Cases not fit for duty transferred to No. 4 Stationary Hospital.	C.R.M.
"	7/5/19		Nil.	C.R.M.
"	8/5/19		Nil.	C.R.M.

"95TH FIELD AMBULANCE"

WAR DIARY or INTELLIGENCE SUMMARY

Army Form C. 2118

Place	Date	Hour	Summary of Events and Information	Remarks and references to Appendices
MALASSISE.	20/5/19		6 O.R.s, R.A.S.C., H.T. Drivers proceeded to No. 5 Area H.T. Vehicle Reception Park, 257 Company, R.A.S.C., St Andre.	CRM
"	21/5/19		Transport Wagons and Ordnance Equipment proceeded by road to be handed in at Ordnance Depot, Beaumarais, Calais, under instructions received from H.Q. 31st Division.	CRM
"	22/5/19		nil.	CRM
"	23/5/19		nil.	CRM
"	24/5/19		8 O.R., R.A.M.C. Transferred to No. 10 Stationary Hospital for duty. 7 O.R., R.A.M.C. Transferred to No. 11 C.C.S. for duty. 2 O.R., R.A.S.C., H.T. Transferred to No. 5 Area H.T. Vehicle Reception Park, St Andre, for duty.	CRM
"	25/5/19		1 O.R., R.A.S.C., H.T. proceeded to England for demobilisation.	CRM
"	26/5/19		3 O.R., R.A.S.C., M.T. proceeded to No. 10 Vehicle Reception Park, St Omer, with one lorry, one "Sunbeam" and two Ford Ambulance Cars.	CRM

95TH FIELD AMBULANCE

Army Form C. 2118

WAR DIARY
or
INTELLIGENCE SUMMARY
(Erase heading not required.)

Instructions regarding War Diaries and Intelligence Summaries are contained in F.S. Regs., Part II. and the Staff Manual respectively. Title Pages will be prepared in manuscript.

Place	Date	Hour	Summary of Events and Information	Remarks and references to Appendices
MALAISE.	27/5/19.		nil.	CRM.
"	28/5/19.		nil.	CRM.
"	29/5/19.		No. 39489. Sgt. Major Cly. Gurgan, R.A.M.C. proceeded to England for demobilisation.	CRM.
"	30/5/19.		nil.	CRM.
"	31/5/19.		Orders received from A.D.M.S. 5th Area, for all other Ranks, R.A.M.C. on strength to proceed to No. 11 C.C.S. Steinwerck immediately.	CRM.
			Capt. C.E. Theron, R.A.M.C. granted 30 days leave to U.K. To report to No. 39 Stationary Hospital for duty on expiration of leave.	CRM.

C.R. Menyou
Capt. R.A.M.C.
COMMANDING
95TH FIELD AMBULANCE.

95TH
FIELD
AMBULANCE.
No..............
Date 31/5/19.

www.ingramcontent.com/pod-product-compliance
Lightning Source LLC
Chambersburg PA
CBHW081406160426
43193CB00013B/2118